The Perfect Imperfect Me!

From Hopeless and Helpless to Happy and Healthy

A RECOVERY FROM ANOREXIA

HEATHER COBURN

www.theperfectimperfectme.com

Library and Archives Canada Cataloguing in Publication

Coburn, Heather, 1972–

    The perfect imperfect me! : from hopeless and helpless to happy and healthy / Heather Coburn.

ISBN 978-1-77136-114-9

1. Coburn, Heather, 1972–. 2. Anorexia nervosa—Patients—Biography. I. Title.

RC552.A5C63 2012   616.85'2620092   C2012-907541-8

Editor: Susan Chilton
Book Cover and Interior Design and Layout: Kim Monteforte, WeMakeBooks.ca
Cover Photograph: Jeff Carlson
Cover Styling: Julianne Costigan and Donna Bogdanus
Proofreaders: Susan Koswan, Hina Parmar

Dedicated to my mentor, Jennifer Brighton,
who genuinely believed in me and gently guided
me along the path to happiness and health.

Table of Contents

This book was made possible with the invaluable help of my editor, Susan Chilton. She turned my personal therapy sessions into a flowing and humorous book, and stood by me through the entire process, not only as an impeccable editor but as an amazing friend. I have learned so much from Susan and cannot thank her enough!

Prologue

••••••••••••••••••••••••••••••••••••••

"CHAMPION" TO UTTERLY DEFEATED

It's August 1988, and I've just won the Girls Under 16 Canadian National Tennis Championship. I'm on cloud nine. My athletic strength, determination and desire to achieve worked! But something within me is not working.

I am lost. I need help. I can no longer function.

The skills I had nurtured to excel in sports through rigid discipline are turning on me and have evolved into a disease that has me firmly by the throat. It is strangling any semblance of who I am. I am severely emaciated and I cannot think straight anymore. People close to me are concerned, saying that my appearance is shocking. They are asking where the fun, bubbly, confident Heather has gone. I wish I knew. I miss her, too. I thought losing weight would make me feel better. But ironically, along with the weight, I lost my health and self-esteem.

My obsession with being thin is becoming what the doctor said it would: a life-threatening illness that is taking everything away from me. I think incessantly about food; I crave it, but at the same time I hate it. I cannot escape my circular thinking. Common sense tells me I need to eat like everyone else, but my mind won't let me. I know I am paper thin but I just cannot change the daily routine that is making me sicker and sicker. Round and round I go. I have no life anymore. Everything I love is slipping away from me. I have lost my passion for anything and everything.

My plan has backfired. I've lost my spark.

I, Robot

● ●

MORNING

Healthy Heather is missing in action. I open my eyes and see that the fluorescent red lights of my alarm clock read 6:15. What day is it? Oh yeah, Monday. Great. I'm disappointed already and I've been awake for all of three seconds. I brush my teeth, put on my workout clothes and drive to the gym. On the way, I look down at what is, to me, a bulge in my stomach and I think, "I feel fat."

I step onto the treadmill that is my second home and pound away. Today I'll run for forty-five minutes to burn enough calories to work off that darn piece of birthday cake and side of ice cream that I ate last night. Oh, why didn't I have the willpower to just say no? Then I could still be snoozing peacefully, like most people are at this hour.

I am surrounded by others, though, who do have the same morning routine of working out. I know most of them but I don't care about anyone. All I can focus on right now is burning off those hideous, empty calories. I don't dare think of anything else; nothing could be more important at this moment. How I long for the day when I didn't even know what a calorie was. Now these tiny units of measure dictate my entire existence.

I'm five-foot-five and live in fear of my weight hitting anything near triple digits.

Finally, what feels like an eternity is over. Calories burned. I'm physically tired and already planning for my return at five this afternoon when I'll work off whatever I end up eating today. But of course, I'll do my best to keep that to a minimum.

I shower, ignore the ladies in the change room and do up my pants. They feel tight. Looks like I'll be running for another forty-five minutes after work no matter what I eat or don't eat today. I walk with my head down into Starbucks, get my coffee and leave. I didn't even consider glancing up at the girl who kindly took my order and wished me a good day. I get to work, sit down and see two co-workers chatting. Are they talking about me? I check my BlackBerry. No new messages. My heart sinks. I feel lonely and empty inside.

AFTERNOON

It's finally lunchtime. I'm starving as breakfast consisted of almost nothing—eating more would have made me feel fatter than I already did. People tell me that fat is not a feeling. Well, I beg to differ. I say it belongs right up there on the list: happy, sad, fat. Makes sense to me.

What to eat for lunch, what not to eat for lunch. Seems like the biggest decision I've had to make in my entire life. Calorie, calorie, calorie (the only information currently stored in my brain). I grab a salad (this makes me feel strangely powerful) and park myself back at my desk waiting for the work day to inch to an end. It's 12:10 p.m.

EVENING

Finally 5 p.m. arrives, after what seemed like another eternity. The last thing I want to do is to go back to my home away from home, the dreaded treadmill. But I don't give myself a choice. Again forty-five minutes feels like forever. Oh, this is so hard; I'm totally exhausted, both physically and mentally.

I arrive home at 6:30, dinnertime. I'm starving and the food battle raging in my head since I woke up twelve hours ago has not subsided. How many calories have I had today and how many do I have left? I dream back to the day when my eating was based on hunger cues. I pull my low-fat dinner out of the microwave and it tastes terrible. I'm not satisfied. All I want to do is to fall asleep. This day has been way too painful.

As I lie down, I realize that today I have not looked one single person in the eye or cracked one smile. And that is not atypical. Any semblance of who I once was has vanished. I suddenly realize what the first three letters of "diet" spell.

Of course, I cannot fall asleep. The fact that I'm starving wins out over the "die, die, die" that's now echoing in my brain. I go downstairs and in absolute misery polish off two rows of cookies. I reset my alarm for 6:15 again. I have to work off those cookies. Tomorrow, I'll relive today, like some sort of pre-programmed, powerless robot. I fall asleep feeling fat and alone.

How did I get here? Who am I? Is this ever going to end?

Life has no value for me. It's just one big struggle. I'm in my own private war zone all because of this horrible disease—my eating disorder! It has taken absolutely everything away from me. I recognize that. With each day that passes, I grow more and more scared. Petrified, really, unable to move. Inside, I can feel my heart fluttering; I'm often dizzy and cold.

At last, after much pleading and not for the first time, my loving sister and devoted mother convince me to check myself into the hospital.

I need to turn my life over to the medical professionals. Again.

Salvation?

●●●●●●●●●●●●●●●●●●●●●●●●●●●●●●●●●●●

I'm watching everything through sharp, focused eyes as I sit here on yet another bed in yet another hospital. I see a woman walking down the hall toward my room. She is dressed smartly, looks confident and has an easy smile. She must be staff.

"Hello, Heather. My name is Jennifer Brighton. I'm going to be your primary worker while you are here in the eating-disorder clinic."

She glances at the picture on my nightstand. I explain, "Everyone keeps asking if that's my sister, but it's actually me a very long time ago. That's what I looked like before this illness took control of my life."

"Wow, Heather, you look so beautiful!" she replies, warmly.

My heart sinks, seriously doubting that I'll ever get my life back, let alone that healthy, smiling, round, former face of mine. This lady has no idea that this illness has tied me up in a straitjacket since I was in my teens.

"How much experience do you have?" I blurt out rudely, not thinking of anything other than that I need an expert who "gets" this disease, if I'm to have any hope at all.

She smiles while pulling up a chair. "I have more experience than you know, Heather, and it's most important that you develop a rapport and trust with me and the rest of the staff so that we can all assist you with your recovery."

Recovery? I'm tentative, scared and, at thirty-five, not the least bit convinced that is remotely possible.

Pop Goes the Diet

● ●

Being in a hospital is always the most threatening experience I endure. My sole source of self-esteem is that I have the power to stay at an unhealthy low weight, so to be told to stop exercising and start gaining is devastating. I am completely blind to the fact that these people are trying to help me get my life back so I fight against them every step of the way.

I am not alone here; there are ten other women and one man in treatment with me. It is heartbreaking to see all these beautiful people tortured like this. Yet at the same time, when we stand back and listen to ourselves, we can almost laugh at our nonsensical thought processes.

I sit down to lunch on "pop day." I hate pop, unless of course it is diet. But the clinic staff members are savvy and they know if we are deviating from the meal plan, which includes regular pop. They are tough on us. Today, there is someone sitting in for the normal dietician and, boy, are we ready to pounce on her! A supply teacher!

Not one of us says a word but we all know what the others are thinking. While she goes out to check on something, we dive into our covert, diet-friendly knapsacks, placed inconspicuously under the table, exchange the real pop for diet pop and dump the butter packs from our trays. We range in age from seventeen to fifty-five, and our giggles permeate the room.

After a hospital meal, we have "sit time," and on this day, it takes on a whole new meaning. After the twenty minutes it takes us to have our butterless lunch and our (diet) pop, we sit there like little schoolgirls feeling guilty about what we just did. Every face is solemn because at this precise moment we realize just how disordered our eating and thinking really are. Why does a regular-calorie pop or a tiny package of butter bother us so much?

During sit time, we are expected to express how we are doing. On this day the air is heavy, the conversation minimal and the silence deafening. Instead of sitting, we're slinking down into our chairs. We've been naughty, but we've only hurt ourselves. Even we can see it. Life is definitely going off the rails.

Enough. It's time to try to get back on track.

Heather Coburn, C'mon Down!

Six months have passed in a blink of an eye. In fact, these eyes of mine have never cried so much. I have come a long way, but I still long for the life that I know I am meant to enjoy. I have everything: a wonderful family, a great job as an accountant, a beautiful home and true friends who have stood by me through everything. But today, my hospital stay is over. How am I going to survive out there? I am terrified. I desperately do not want to go down the agonizing path of anorexia again but I know all too well how easy it is to relapse.

Twice before I've been discharged, and twice before my weight kept dropping until I was re-admitted. Just entertaining this memory makes me feel sick to my stomach. There is nothing worse than this damn eating disorder. In fact, when I got divorced, I said to my sister, "This is a piece of cake compared to anorexia." She was totally shocked. I was being totally truthful.

I know that my astute doctor recognizes my fear and desperation. Without me even asking, he hands me Jennifer's private practice information. Thank God. Jennifer has been invaluable during my inpatient treatment. Every week she has taught me life lessons that actually work. The doctor reminds me that individual therapy is not provided in the hospital program and that private help will cost a pretty penny, because public health care does not cover these services. However, in order for me to maintain my gains, research indicates that weekly therapy for at least a year will be necessary.

Yikes!

Nonetheless, I know in my heart that without continued therapy I will digress and I do not want history to repeat itself a third time. I don't need Bob Barker to tell me that "The Price is Right," whatever it is. I never want to go down this excruciating path again. I would rather be hit by a Mack Truck. I book Jennifer's first available appointment.

Life 101

● ●

I have received therapy from what feels like a gazillion "experts," with little or no success. I catch on fast and am intimately acquainted with a prescriptive, simple formula: eat this much, gain this much, maintain it... eat, gain, maintain. Eat, gain, maintain. I hear it over and over again. No matter what details I tell them about my life or inner struggles, they sympathetically deliver their standard line: just get to and stay at a BMI of 20, and you'll be cured.

Well, it's not that easy. Sure I can gain the weight for a while, but that always ends up making me feel ten times worse. Therapists generally parrot back or paraphrase whatever I say and I feel it's predictable and a waste of my time.

Then, in walked fate. Actually, in walked Jennifer. I knew this therapy was going to work the first time I experienced Jennifer's fresh and insightful approach. I look forward to our sessions because I know that we do some really hard, relevant work and then she lightens it up and sends me away with something to focus on. She has me explore different solutions to my own difficulties, while posing questions that may guide my thinking in the right directions. To top it off, she adds a few suggestions of her own. It's like taking Life 101 to set you on the right course.

Most importantly, I am able to be one hundred percent honest with her. It is the first time I feel someone respects the fact that I have all of the book knowledge to get better and also knows that what I really need is someone to support me through thick and thin, so to speak, and not make me feel bad, guilty or ashamed when I regress. Others have made me feel they are impatient, frustrated and even angered by my illness. It's as though they think I can just listen to their advice and turn on the light bulb. But it's nothing like that. I need a genuinely understanding, knowledgeable person who can gently challenge and guide me. Jennifer has me laughing and crying all in one sitting. Jennifer is "real."

Formulas, Please

•••••••••••••••••••••••••••••••••••

I do what you do in a waiting room—wait.

"Heather."

There she is, at the door. I instantly feel a sense of calmness wash over me as a sincere smile spreads across my face. This is surprising to me and feels unexpectedly reassuring. I have a teammate to help me and I need one! It is my first appointment with Jennifer since my tough hospital stay. Today, all I care about is maintaining my weight and staying well. Surprisingly, I am pretty comfortable with my new body. I'm not emaciated anymore; I feel healthy and I even have a hint of my round, chipmunk cheeks back. However, I am paranoid that the whirlpool of anorexia will suck me under again as it has in the past. This time I am going to take every precaution. My only lifeline is this therapy with someone I'm entrusting with everything.

Jennifer welcomes me into her corner office and appears at ease in her comfortable chair. I can feel my heart beating a mile a minute. This room is cozy but it's definitely a typical therapist's office staged to try and make me feel at home. I'm feeling scared, vulnerable and incompetent. Only weak people need this kind of help. Why don't I have the strength to just be happy and normal like everyone else?

I see a bulletin board on the wall with a quote: "Life is what happens to you while you're busy making other plans." John Lennon. No kidding, John. I'm never in the moment. I'm always planning for later, whether it's later in the day or later in life. I'm totally missing out on the moments that make up my life. Jennifer obviously selected this Lennon quote herself and it really hits home for me.

"Jennifer, I need you to give me the formula for staying healthy. But not the old eat, gain, maintain mantra."

As I say this, I'm thinking she can teach me the other formulas for life in other sessions. I need equations and I need one now. That's the only way I know how to work; I'm an accountant, for heaven's sake! Equipped with a pad of paper and a pen to jot down every single word of wisdom, I am filled with questions.

"What do I do, Jennifer?" Beneath some optimism, I remain lost and unsure of myself.

She says, "First, put down your pen and pad, Heather, and just be here with me right now."

I think, oh please, lady, please don't make me put them down. But out of respect, I place them right beside my leg in the hope that I can somehow pick them up without her noticing.

"You know what to do," she continues. "You've been eating properly for six months now. We don't need to go over your meal plan; just follow it. I know you can do it!"

I know you can do it? Did she just say that with total confidence? I am so struck by this, the impact makes me reel. Despite knowing the slippery slope that has been my history, Jennifer actually believes in me. She has faith in me. Astonishing!

When I met Jennifer in the hospital, I saw how she worked. Somehow she has mastered the art of being tough with patients while still being kind. I didn't know people could do that. She "tells it like it is" and is extremely knowledgeable, but also has fun ways to coax out insights. In short, she just "gets" it. She gets "us." I know Jennifer doesn't beat around the bush. For the first time, I think I might actually be able to do this. I can physically feel a bit of my anxiety melt away. With a grin, I discreetly pick up my pad and write, "Formula One: Continue to follow my meal plan." Maybe she is right and I can do this. Geez, this isn't rocket science!

So why do I feel we have lift-off?

Baby Steps

● ●

I'm pretty excited about seeing Jennifer again. It's our second appointment and I have been successful at eating properly and following her instructions to the letter. Jennifer's confidence in me from last week's session definitely caused me to stay on track, because I sure don't believe in myself.

She appears at the door. Seeing her, the biggest smile crosses mine and it feels so good! I jump up with a newfound sense of hope. "Heather," she calls.

"Right here."

We go back into her office and she asks how my week was.

I don't even think to ask her how her week was as I'm too consumed with myself. I reply, "Awesome! I've maintained my weight."

"How do you know that?" she inquires politely.

"Because I weigh myself every day." Doesn't everyone?

"Do you think you really need to be doing that? If

you make sure you eat properly, your weight will take care of itself. Heather, what would it be like to get rid of the scale?"

Get rid of the scale? Is she serious? Baby steps, lady, baby steps! I've been weighing myself daily for the past twenty-two years and you expect me to just stop cold turkey? It's what makes me feel in control of my life. If I weigh more one day, I'm upset and I eat less. If I weigh less the next day, I'm happy. My weight dictates how I feel and what I eat or don't eat and yes, mainly don't eat. It's as simple as that. I am so not ready to step off that scale. I hope I don't look as threatened as I feel.

"Well, Jennifer," I answer slowly, pretending I'm mulling it over, "I'm so concerned about my weight right now that I'm not quite prepared to do that."

She nods. "Could we think of an experiment? For instance, how about you hand your scale over to me for one week and if you can't handle it, I promise I'll give it back to you."

Oh dear, oh dear, oh dear. What to do, what to do? Do I feel heart palpitations? This woman is trying to help me but with every fibre of my being, I do not want to do this. Finally, I respond, "All right, I'll bring it next week—but I am not happy about it!" What's the point of lying to her? I want her to help me, so I tell the truth.

She laughs. "I don't expect that you are, but it's possible that with a little short-term discomfort you might reap long-term gains."

Not "Spinning" Out of Control

● ●

A week has passed. I've weighed the idea of taking in the scale but I know in my heart I'll just go out and buy a new one. (Hmm… They have new ones that talk to you.) The scale is the power button in my robotic world. It can turn me on or off the world. This time around, though, I really want to recover so I don't want to lie or fake any of my feelings. I absolutely want to recover so I don't want to lie or fake any of my feelings. I absolutely want Jennifer to help me and so far, when I've told her the truth, even when I know it's not what she wants to hear, she has accepted it. I decide she won't desert me if I tell her I simply cannot give up my soulmate, the scale.

She calls me in.

It's amazing how the smile on her face lets me know that I'm not alone and gives me more strength than I've ever felt. Jennifer really does listen. I've always felt pressured to tell other professionals what they wanted to hear for fear of what their reactions would be. I was afraid that they would judge me or tell me, in a harsh manner, that I wasn't "doing it right." I never want to hear that phrase again because it triggers hopelessness. I can freely tell Jennifer the good, the bad and the really ugly.

It boggles my mind, actually, that eating-disorder treatment can feel as rigid and unforgiving as the illness itself. I can start to feel like I'm locked in a power struggle rather than a slow and steady integration of a healthier way of living. I didn't become anorexic overnight; there is no quick, easy or foolproof fix. One XXS size does not fit all. Jennifer is someone who will highlight what is healthy and what is not, but she will not judge or reject me if I am not ready to make a change. I feel sure that I can tell her anything.

As I take my seat, I also take a deep breath, and decide to drop a bomb. "Jennifer, uhh, I've gone to spin class with my friends a few times."

She doesn't even flinch. Instead, she looks up at me with openness and says, "I'm glad you told me that, Heather."

Wow, that was easy! I was a little bit worried that she might lose it, as others have before her. Jennifer is the first person who has helped me who knows exactly where I am at. That brings me such peace.

"How might your doctor react if he knew this?"

"He might be concerned," I admit.

"Why?"

"Well, I'm supposed to lay off exercise. He might think I'm 'spinning' out of control," I joke feebly.

Jennifer smiles. "Ultimately, this is your decision. I know it seems odd that you've been asked to stop exercising when everyone else is encouraged to pursue it wholeheartedly, but remember that when you have an eating disorder, exercise is often another symptom. You know: calories in, calories out."

"I do remember that it's really best to integrate exercise slowly back into my daily routine, yes. Thanks for reminding me. But it's hard. I miss working out."

"It's just until you've gotten past the riskier stages of recovery and you can reliably maintain your weight," Jennifer says kindly. "It's not forever."

Phew! Oh, how nice to be treated like an adult rather than be scolded. Jennifer laid out the facts but did not show any anger. So I can be entirely truthful! I feel relief and Jennifer sees it. She turns to a few minutes of light conversation during which she says, "So, Heather, I see that you didn't bring your scale."

Fully at ease now, I have to laugh. "I know! I couldn't do it!"

"It's okay. How about you try and not weigh yourself for just one day this week?"

That seems manageable. "I can do that."

"That's fantastic, Heather," she says. "Eliminating behaviours or routines that feel so significant is difficult. If I had asked you to eliminate one day of weighing at the outset, you would have thought that was impossible. But by thinking of going a full week without it, you were able to see what small changes you really are capable of. You have a tendency to set your sights very high, which unfortunately is not always achievable. I'm glad to see that you were again honest, forthright and willing to work with me. We truly are making progress, one small but mighty step at a time."

The very next day, I sidestep my soulmate. I'm dying to tell Jennifer so I send her a quick email simply saying: "Success!"

She gets right back to me with the words that already mean so much to me: *I knew you could do it!*

Crazy Theory

● ●

"Jennifer, I was invited to a party!" I blurt out at our next appointment.

"Did you go?"

"Yes. It was a no-brainer. I remember my sister Sonja telling me that if you get invited to something and you say no, they may not ask you again, so say yes and the invitations will keep on coming. I took her advice this time and went. I had a wonderful night! My friends actually made fun of me and I enjoyed the light-hearted attention. While I was in the washroom, my food arrived. I had ordered a large plate of caesar salad and a chicken bacon burger. My friends said that while I was gone, they were wondering if there was any possible way I would ever eat even half of it. I laughed and told them that I am no longer on a mission to lose weight; it sure didn't work for me before!"

Jennifer chuckles.

I go on. "I ate more than half; I ate everything on the

plate! They were so impressed, they all chipped in and bought me a drink! A dessert was too expensive, I guess," I joke.

"Heather, that is great," Jennifer enthuses. "What was that whole experience like for you?"

"The positive attention and social involvement with work friends felt wonderful, Jennifer. I was actually in the moment." That's true, but the "new me" is always honest with my therapist, so I continue. "But I felt insecure and still do. I'm not very confident in myself."

"You could try a little trick that might help with that," she suggests.

"Does it involve a second Smirnoff?" I kid. "No, seriously, that's awesome! I can't wait to hear it."

"It's a theory called, 'Fake it until you make it' or 'Act as if.'"

This sounds pretty weird but I better listen, so I say politely, "I have no idea what you are talking about."

"Let's try it right now." She looks at me encouragingly. "It's easy. Think of the gathering you were at and pretend for a moment that you feel really good about yourself. Imagine you know what you are doing and you feel confident in the environment and with these peers. Just stay with that for a moment."

I start to imagine the whole evening and in my mind's eye I can see that I would be more relaxed, sit differently and not try so hard. In short, I can see where she is going with this; I'm not confident and I show it on the outside and this is not helping the matter.

"If you do it long enough and stick with it," Jennifer continues, "you will start to see that you have these capacities and you will begin to believe in yourself. 'Act as if' you are this way and it will become second nature. Eventually, it will be the real you."

I'm skeptical, but I don't say so. She hasn't steered me wrong so far. I leave with some reservations about this crazy theory but what the heck. I decide to give it a shot.

Suspension Bridge

Today I step on the scale and to my horror, for the first time since regaining my health, I see a slight drop in my weight. I am terrified of relapse. Staring down at the number in abject horror, I break out in a clammy sweat.

Can the damn disease be circling back for me yet again?

There are three long days before I see Jennifer again. I decide the only thing I can do is ignore the drop for now. I keep repeating to myself that I'm not going to have to battle my old foe again, but I'm not convinced. I'm scared and strangely exhausted. I spend the next few days totally out of sorts, trying to fight off my anxiety. I feel dread, I feel impending disaster, I feel doomed.

Monday finally rolls around. I enter Jennifer's office, literally shaking. "Jennifer, I am so frightened. My weight has dropped." My voice is hollow and desperate.

"Okay," she replies serenely. "Is the reason you are so scared right now strictly because of your weight?"

"Yes! I've dropped two pounds since last week and I can feel a relapse creeping up on me. I've blown it."

"Heather, you are only looking at one piece of the puzzle. Your weight is only one part of your recovery and you have been able to maintain it for two months now. A drop of two pounds does not need to throw you like this. It does not mean that you have to go back to your old, bad habits."

"It doesn't?" I feel an ever-so-slight lightening. I know that my doctor is very weight-driven and if I told him this he would flip his lid, so I'm shocked by Jennifer's response.

"You have been progressing extremely well in all aspects of your recovery and weight is only one of them. Health is not just one specific item; it's many. Emotionally, you have been stable and secure. Socially, you have been enjoying your family and friends. Physically, you are healthy and you are holding up a full-time job just fine. You are cherishing life, and that is wonderful. These two pounds that you are focusing on are only one small piece of a much larger puzzle."

"But, Jennifer, I'm absolutely terrified. What do I do?" It is still hard for me to digest her calm and confidence because I'm so frightened.

"Have you ever been on a suspension bridge, Heather?"

"Yes, in Vancouver."

"Do you remember the feeling of being right in the middle of it?"

"Yes! I was scared you-know-what-less!"

"And what did you do to get rid of that feeling?"

"I walked to the other side."

"Then do the same thing here: Walk yourself to safety."

"But how?"

"You know how."

"I do?"

"Yes."

"Please, Jennifer, just tell me. You have no idea how horrible these past few days have been. I have been so scared and preoccupied."

"Heather, when you hear the words coming out of your own mouth, they will have more meaning. So you tell me what you have to do. I know that you are more than capable of that."

"Eat properly, make eating properly a priority and most of all, believe in myself."

"Exactly! Now to help ease your anxiety, let's review your meal plan for the next week."

We spend the next half hour going through all of my meals for the next seven days. We choose things that I enjoy and that are convenient. Jennifer makes it easy. We work together.

"Now, Heather, focus on all of the gains that you have made and be diligent with your eating. I know you can do this."

Did she just say that again? My stress lifts, my mind

clears, and I stand up to leave firmly on my feet again. I have what might be only a teensy-weensy bit of confidence in myself but, boy, after the last seventy-five hours, does it ever feel good.

Mirror, Mirror

• •

A few weeks go by. I've stayed focused on the basics of tending to my health. I don't feel alone and this gives me so much more strength. However, something is bothering me today and I'm in a tizzy. I wonder if Jennifer can figure me out this time, because I sure can't.

"Jennifer, I met a guy that I've gone on a few dates with." I pause, uncomfortably.

"Yes?" She looks at me inquisitively.

"Well, he's driving me crazy!"

This elicits a barrel of laughs from both of us.

"Why is that?" she probes.

"He's not uplifting to me. He's constantly asking me questions and questioning himself too, and I hate it."

She invites me to give her an example. I have one readily at hand.

"Well, I dropped him off while I ran some errands and when I went to pick him up only an hour later, he asked me if I missed him. He asked it like he was serious and it was a total turn-off. He was just so unsure of himself."

Jennifer thinks for a second. "Heather, do you remember when you felt unsure of yourself? It wasn't too long ago."

"Yes," I admit.

"Well, you just observed your mirror reflection. You are seeing your old insecurities and it doesn't look good or feel nice, does it?"

"No," I say flatly. Inside, I am pondering. I know she's right, but I tend to think that everyone else has their lives together and that I am the only person who ever feels insecure. How could this good-looking, athletic thirty-something guy be unsure of himself?

"You have been questioning yourself throughout your recovery, so it's unlikely that you will want to deal with these characteristics in another person. Can you see that, Heather?"

I totally can. Seeing this lack of self-esteem in some-one else really turned me off. "Yes," I concur. "And I guess that's why when I was like that, nobody liked it either."

"It looks like you've made some progress, Heather! You've faked it until you made it! You are genuinely feeling good about yourself now."

Jennifer is right and does it ever feel good! Maybe that theory wasn't so crazy after all.

"You need to surround yourself with people who are positive and who have a positive impact on you," she declares to me. "Do you think this guy can?"

Umm, nope. There are plenty of other fish in the sea. I need a strong swimmer. And best of all, I'm starting to think I deserve one.

The Answer to π

• •

I'm enjoying a Sunday night dinner with my family and my mom serves one of her sinfully good apple pies for dessert. It's my favourite and I haven't had it in ages! I dig into my piece feeling like I've died and gone to heaven, so my mom asks if I'd like to take some home with me. What an excellent idea! I'll have some for tomorrow. She sends me home with my lovingly sealed care package. Aren't moms great?

I can't wait to eat more pie tomorrow, I muse in the car. I get home and this scrumptious pie leads me to temptation. I'll just take one bite tonight. I take a bite. Well, maybe one more bite. Okay, one more can't hurt. I force myself to put the rest away. What a fantastic treat this will be with lunch! But before I go to bed, I hear the pie calling out to me from the fridge. Uh-oh. I go just to take a peek, then a nibble, then a rather large bite, and then I polish off the pie, feeling guilt-ridden. *Arrrggh...*

I wake up the next morning feeling "crumby," just as crumby as last night's pie. I am bloated and full of regret. I go to work, where I can't concentrate. I'm still focusing on the too-much-of-a-good-thing fiasco of last night. Thank goodness it's Monday, my appointment day, so I get to bounce this problem off Jennifer. I hope she has a solution because this freakin' pie is ruining my day.

"Jennifer, I am so stressed, I can't focus. Last night, I ate three pieces of apple pie."

She raises an eyebrow. "Why did you do that, Heather?"

"Because it was amazing pie! I enjoyed a piece at my mom's and then I took two pieces home. But then I kept picking at them all night until they were gone. I didn't even enjoy them because I was battling in my head not to eat them!"

"How often does something like this happen?"

I confess. "Probably once a month."

"Ironically, Heather, yesterday I went to a baby shower and pretty much ate all afternoon!" Jennifer grins. That puts the first smile of the day on my face. "Am I going to worry about it all day today?" she asks, rhetorically. "No. That would definitely not be helpful. Am I going to eat properly today like I normally do? Yes, I am. It's really that simple!"

She laughs and I do, too. But then I wonder why she can move on and be happy today while I am consumed by guilt and worry. That's not fair!

"But I can't stop obsessing about it, Jennifer," I acknowledge, sadly. "It's literally all I have thought about today."

"I can see that," she answers, sympathetically. "Ask yourself this question: Is it going to help you to spend the entire day today distracted by apple pie that you ate yesterday?"

"No. It's making me miserable." I feel tears stinging at the back of my eyes.

"Then why are you doing it?"

"I have done this for years. Whenever I don't feel good about my weight or what I have eaten, I focus on it and I torture myself. I beat myself up about it. It sounds so weird now that I say it to you! Who wants to voluntarily beat herself up? Look at you; you ate more yesterday than usual, but today you are happy, feeling totally sin-free. Obviously, I've been on the wrong track with this one."

I'm expecting Jennifer to say "Duh!" but she politely reflects, "Perspective is everything, Heather. Indulging once in a while is normal—welcome to the world of normal! Getting caught up in self-deprecating thoughts is not going to help you feel better."

That makes sense! I like the sound of "normal."

"Heather, how could you help yourself feel better right now?"

Good question, I think to myself. I sense a lesson coming.

"Try to imagine that your uncomfortable feelings are like waves cascading over you. They will peak and subside; you just need to ride them out. The waves will roll out of sight and all will return to normal."

I have to give this some thought. Visualizing. Hmm. My brain really is not wired to think like this. I suspect I lost the entire right side somewhere; I need a logical, mathematical approach. If my journey has taught me one thing, it's that things that might sound easy for others are generally not easy for me.

Still... "I'll give it a try," I agree.

I guess I have to keep up my part of the equation.

My Closet Overfloweth

● ●

I've gone shopping—oh yes, have I ever! It's not that I don't have enough clothes already; my closets are stuffed and spilling over. But I'll make room in my garden shed if I have to because I don't believe anyone can ever have too many clothes. I'm shopping online now, too, where stores are open 24/7 and outfits are but a quick click away. I make the girl in the Shopaholic books look like an amateur. I know that I have far too many clothes (to say nothing of handbags), yet I continue to buy more. More, more, more—the opposite of my long-time approach to food.

My mother asked me this week, "How many pairs of golf shoes do you have, Heather?"

I underplay it. "Oh, about ten." Actually, it may be twelve, perhaps fifteen, I'm pretty sure no more than twenty, but I don't want to get into too much trouble.

Mom answered, "I have two pairs and that is plenty."

I know she is right but when there is something I want, I have to have it. However, it never ends; there is always something more that I must have or I simply can't go on.

"Heather," Jennifer calls me in. I can't wait to show her my new Coach purse and wallet, my new Anne Klein skirt and matching top, and oh yes, my new pair of Nine West shoes. (Hey, it's not like I have no restraint; they're not Louboutins.)

"How was your trip?" Jennifer asks.

"Great! I was just in Atlanta visiting friends for the long weekend. Look at all of the cool stuff I got!" I mimic a little walk down the runway.

"Very nice," she nods. "Didn't you have a new outfit on last week, and the week before that?"

"Yes," I boast. "I'm having so much fun shopping that I'm running out of room in my house." Maybe I imagine the look Jennifer gives me, but suddenly I don't feel right about this. Something inside me is telling me that all of the "stuff" I have is excessive. I shake it off. I justify, I'm doing well at this recovery process, so I deserve to splurge. Oh yeah, baby.

"Did you have fun with your friends?" Jennifer asks.

"For sure! You should see their house!" I am pumped. "They live in a gated community. They have a swimming pool and trampoline in their backyard—a backyard that backs onto a golf course! They even have to talk to each other by intercom in their house, it's so big!"

Jennifer patiently asks again about the people I had gone to visit. "And how were your friends, Heather?"

What? Did I not mention them yet? "Great," I reply, obliviously. "They have the life."

Jennifer is silent, so I know something is up. "Why is it so important to you that these people have so much money?" she begins. "And why is it so important for you to have all of these designer outfits?"

I know that she's getting at something, so I respond from my heart. "I've always thought that it's impressive to have nice outfits and big homes."

"You have come such a long way in your self-development, Heather, but you still look to the outside to feel good about yourself. There's a writer named Dan Pink who talks about how focusing on external rewards like money, trips and cars kills the ability to think out of the box and be creative. Material goods don't feed the soul; self-trust, life meaning and purpose do. Simply put, it's the things inside of you, not what's worn on your back, that will give you true pleasure. You need to start getting your satisfaction from within. Help me understand why you still don't feel good about you, as you are inside."

She is absolutely correct. I do look to possessions and to other people for approval. I try to think of why this is and, after a few minutes, answer. "Jennifer, while I was sick, I lost myself. I did so many things that I'm ashamed of. I looked dreadful and I behaved in embarrassing ways. I can't ever undo that and I feel a ton of shame that I don't think will ever end. I genuinely fear that I will never, ever again find the confidence I had when I was younger. I've messed up. But I can look good outwardly. I can have the trappings of success, even if I don't feel successful inside."

"Heather, we can definitely work on this. You will reclaim yourself in time."

"I doubt anything will work, Jennifer, but because I trust you, I'll try." How can she possibly find ways to give me that confidence back?

And why, I suddenly wonder, are they called the "trappings" of success?

Repairs

• •

"Heather, I'm going to teach you a few things over the next few weeks that will help you with your lack of confidence issues," Jennifer announces.

Finally, the secrets I've been waiting for.

"First of all, you have a wonderful opportunity in your life right now to make repairs." I can tell she's got something important to share so I lean forward slightly in anticipation. I really want to know how I can possibly redeem myself and get my confidence back, so I listen carefully.

She continues, "There is always a way to make a graceful repair."

"Thank goodness, because my list of repairs is as long as Wayne Gretzky's list of scoring records!" I tease.

Jennifer cracks a smile. "Give me some examples."

"But, Jennifer, but we only have an hour!" One of the nicest things about our relationship is that we can have some fun in therapy; I can tell her anything. So I do.

"Before I came to you, I was so self-involved that I didn't care what I did or how I acted, as long as I got what I wanted. I did the most selfish things that I can now see are totally out of character for me. I would walk with my head down, never look anyone in the eye, and I had absolutely no manners or consideration for others. In some cases, I still don't. For instance, I'll park anywhere."

"Anywhere?" she echoes.

"Anywhere," I repeat firmly. "If I'm going to the grocery store, I take the spot in the fire zone closest to the door. If I'm grabbing a coffee, I leave my car running right outside the door and go in. If I'm at the tennis club, I make my own spot in the no-parking zone right in front of the entrance." I save the worst for last. "I have even been known to use handicapped parking spots."

I actually don't feel reluctant confiding all of this. I've learned by now that Jennifer never judges me.

"Great examples," she says with a laugh. "Now, I'm going to ask you this: Do you think you're above the law?"

"What do you mean?"

"If it was four in the morning and you were at a red light and nobody was around, would you go through it?"

I know she is expecting me to say, "Of course not!" But in my youth, I actually did run a red or two at around that time of the morning, so I say, "Trust me, you don't want to know."

"Obviously we have some work here!" Jennifer is clearly amused. "This week I have two things for you to do, Heather. How about you park strictly in proper parking spaces, and try to be courteous with people? The next time you go to a coffee shop you could park appropriately and, if someone is behind you when you open the door, allow them to go in ahead of you."

"Sounds easy enough," I declare, already worried that the person I ushered in would then be ahead of me in the line-up. "But how is this going to give me confidence?"

"Trust me and be patient, Heather."

On the way out of her office, Jennifer opens the door for me and says, "Have a great week."

For the first time, I realize that she always opens the door for me. So I look her in the eye and say, "Thank you, Jennifer." I leave with my head up and a smile on my face. Meet people's eyes? Hold doors for them? That will help me? Who'd've thunk it.

I Do Have a Golf Handicap...

●●●●●●●●●●●●●●●●●●●●●●●●●●●●●●●●●●●

As always, I'm keyed up for my therapy appointment today and wondering what new insights and help lie in store.

"So, how was your week?" Jennifer inquires.

"Well, I worked on what we talked about last week." I'm not saying this to please her; I'm saying this to tell her that I actually did and quite liked the results. "I opened the door for people getting coffee, for people at the tennis club and for people at work."

"And?" she prompts.

"It was awesome, Jennifer, absolutely awesome." I mean it. "When I opened the door for an older man at Starbucks, I looked at him and he smiled at me! It was so cute, and he smiled even more when I smiled back. You are not going to believe this, but I even let him go ahead of me in line. Normally, I'm dashing to be in front, but this time I could feel myself pause, breathe and shift my attention to letting him go first. That consciousness helped me slow down, take courteous actions and enjoy the moment. Then, I opened the door for a really cute guy at the tennis club. And guess what?"

Jennifer laughs, revelling in my enthusiasm.

"He winked at me when I let him in ahead of me! So I winked back at him and we both giggled! I had no idea that opening the door for people could be so much fun. Do you have any more tricks like this up your sleeve?"

I'm discovering that I love this feeling of connecting with people and I'm craving more and more of it. This opening-the-door thing ended up being pretty cool.

"Yes, I do," she affirms to my delight. "In fact, it occurred to me that you could work on something with your dad. You know how when you go out with your dad you tend to get upset?"

"Yes, because he keeps telling me to calm down or stop rambling. I can't stand it!"

"Well, the next time you see him, start by asking him a question, like how his day was. You get him talking. That will give you some time to calm down and shift the focus away from yourself."

"That's definitely something I can do."

"And how did you manage with the mighty struggle of parking legally, like the rest of us regular folk?" Her sarcasm makes us both smile.

Joking aside, I'm ashamed to admit that a few times I did still make my own personal parking spot. I know I have to tell her the truth so she knows where I am at and can help me. "Jennifer, I did it your way, or I should say the legal way, for a few days. It was nice not to be embarrassed walking into places when I know people just saw me peel up and park in front of a fire hydrant. But there were times when it was just more convenient to park illegally."

Part of me still doesn't care if people see me do something wrong but the larger part of me definitely doesn't feel good about it. I silently conclude that I must be getting a conscience. Wow, that's going to be a nuisance!

"Keep working on it," Jennifer urges, as always without judgment.

Name-Game Shame

•••••••••••••••••••••••••••••••••••

I'm starting to catch myself doing more and more things that don't feel entirely right. I decide to come forward with them at my next appointment.

"Jennifer, I noticed something about myself. Sometimes I feel like I have to name-drop in order to get people to accept me. I know it sounds wrong when I do it, yet I still keep doing it."

"Ahh. A classic example of a narcissistic behaviour."

"Narcissistic? What's that?" Jennifer often uses words that I'm not familiar with. This is one of them, and frankly I don't like the sound of it.

"It means self-love. You want to make yourself feel important so you dress a certain way and you drop names."

"Ouch!" I wince; this hurts. It's true, though. I do want to be viewed as an important person and I do use things or people to that end, even though I don't like that characteristic in others.

"Can you please explain this further?" I'm hoping she means something different because this kind of self-love is not very lovable.

"Narcissism means that you'll make decisions that meet your needs first. It also means that you want people to admire you, and when you're insecure you fall back on shopping for expensive or designer items to regain a good feeling. It's the same characteristic that you show when you think that you're above the law, going through a red light and creating your own parking spots. With your dad, it's when you ramble on about your life without asking about his. And it's about how you feel the need to drop names. Heather, it's hard to see narcissism in ourselves, but you do show some of the traits."

I am crushed. I could burst into tears. This is the polar opposite of how I want to be perceived. I don't want to have a single one of those traits, that is for sure, let alone a long list like this. I am devastated and overwhelmed because this time I really care about something new that I can't buy: I really care about being, or becoming, a good person. I need to turn over a new leaf.

"I'm so sorry, Jennifer," I manage to stammer. "I feel awful." I definitely need to drop the name-dropping thing like a hot potato.

"I understand, Heather. This is tough stuff to hear, but it's also important. This is an opportunity to grow and learn. Sometimes the hardest lessons have to create pain in order for us to realize just how much we want to change. Throughout the next week, just notice when you exhibit these traits, and particularly who you are doing it with. Just slow down and pay attention, Heather. If you long for close friends, then you must be a true friend. If you long for happy relationships, then you must be a fully giving participant. If you want a happy life, then you have to make the choice to live a life focused on happiness. It's compelling when you truly experience your energy being reflected back to you. You see, the energy you exude will grow and be mirrored back to you. So in a very real sense, in the end, this really is all about you."

I'm pretty confused now and I really just want to get out of here because I feel highly uncomfortable and this conversation is emotionally draining. I don't like knowing that I have made all of these mistakes and at this moment, I am not proud of my behaviour. I can't recall the last time I felt this terrible, this low. The only thing I can force out of my mouth is a weak, "Okay," as I fight off my tears.

"You have done a great job, Heather. You are progressing. You are noticing these things and caring about them. Remember, life is about learning and growing," Jennifer consoles me. A few tears escape and trickle down my face as I leave. I know in my heart that Jennifer has seen that I really want to change. She sees that I am noticing things about myself and trying to take action.

But I recognize that it will probably take a long time for other people to perceive me any differently.

I have a gigantic mountain to climb.

It's All About Me

• •

A few days have passed and I've tried to pull myself up by my bootstraps. I've often reminded myself that I'm not climbing Mount Everest alone; I have a Sherpa guide named Jennifer who knows the terrain. I'm going on a date tonight, determined to make a good impression.

I walk into the restaurant and the hostess asks, "Are you Heather?"

"Yes, I am." I smile, knowing that he must be here and has even told the hostess my name. How nice is that?

She leads me through the restaurant onto the outdoor patio. There he is, sitting at a table for two directly beside a waterfall, with a bottle of sparkling water. He looks so relaxed and confident in himself. He stands up and gives me a hug. "Heather, you look beautiful."

My heart melts. I cannot help but be charmed. "That's sweet of you to say," I respond flirtatiously.

We have a drink and then order dinner. I am having

a marvellous time, talking with him and laughing together. Yikes; suddenly it's dark out. Four hours have flown by and it's time to go. "But we haven't talked about you yet," I say as he pulls back my chair.

Oh my God, it's true! I realize for the first time that about ninety percent of the conversation this evening has been about me. Oh no, I always do this. This is terrible! A familiar feeling of anxiety grips me along with a sinking feeling in my stomach.

"No problem," he says, then adds, "I've learned that you should ask others questions about themselves. So I did."

I obviously haven't learned that. My evening goes from delightful to disastrous in three seconds flat. We hug and say goodbye. I lost my chance. I know I won't hear from him again.

After a miserable Sunday, Monday finally rolls around and I can't wait to talk to Jennifer.

"How are you?" she asks.

I cut right to the chase. "I'm really disappointed in myself. I went on a date with someone and I don't think I made a very good impression."

"Uh-oh."

I can see that she is genuinely engaged. "Well, it seemed like we were having a wonderful time—at least, I was. We were out for hours, but right at the end as we said our goodbyes, I realized that we had talked about me the whole time. I didn't find out anything about him!

I felt like such an idiot. Needless to say," I conclude with a sigh, "he hasn't called."

I am eager to hear Jennifer's take. I never again want to act like I did that Saturday.

She breaks the silence. "Why do you think you did that? Why do you think you had to be the focus of the conversation all night?"

The answer doesn't immediately spring to mind. I need to think. I guess this is what they call "digging deeper." I hope it's not as brutal as the tough-love boot camp I found myself in over my narcissism. Wait a minute: Bingo!

"Because I am only focused on myself, I felt I needed to tell him all about me to impress him?" I venture. I scan my memory banks, hoping not to find any "deposits" of names that I dropped.

"Or is it possible that you were a little nervous?"

"Definitely!"

"Perhaps a bit insecure? Heather, that's all normal for a first date. Remember, you don't need to impress anyone. Just be yourself."

"Easier said than done," I comment ruefully. "What do I do to stop myself next time?"

"What do you think you should do next time?"

It's so rare that Jennifer sounds like a typical therapist. Listen, lady, I'm looking for advice here! "I want you to tell me," I demand.

"Slow down. Tell me what you learned on your date, Heather."

"Well, I learned that it felt good to have someone be interested in me and for them to really listen."

"So do you think this guy, or any guy really, might enjoy the same thing? Being listened to?"

"Uh, yes."

"Curiosity is your friend when you're on a date. Just asking questions and listening show that you are genuinely interested in someone and that you really want to get to know him. You can also volley a bit with questions if you feel stuck. You know—what they ask, you ask."

"I wish we'd had this appointment before I went out on the date," I joke with her. We are giggling now because, with so much of what I have learned, I just have to keep reminding myself to do it.

"You know, Jennifer, this reminds me of what the head pro at my golf course says to his staff: Really listening is the most important thing anyone can ever do. This guy is a class act in dealing with people. He has it down pat, but clearly this is a tough one for me."

"So what is the lesson from both the golf pro's advice and our debrief of your date?"

"Well, I've learned, or remembered, that nobody really wants to sit and just listen to someone tell her own story. Most people are more concerned about what's going on in their own lives, not yours. If you constantly talk about yourself, others will get bored and not want to be around you. If you ask them questions, though, and really listen to their answers, they'll see you're interested in them. They'll want to stop and talk to you."

"Aha, a great life lesson!" Jennifer pronounces.

"You know, after my regrettable date, this is really sinking in. I think I'll practise as I run into people today. I'll start with the question you gave me for my dad: 'How was your day today?' I'll work on bringing the conversation back to them and steering it away from me. I will answer anything they ask me, but I'll make sure there's balance."

"Fabulous, Heather!"

"My parents are going to love this lesson! 'No, no, mom and dad, enough about me, what's up with you?' My dad will have to stop accusing me of rambling!" I laugh. "And you know what the truth is? I actually genuinely want to know about them and other people, too."

I feel so much better having talked about this. Jennifer has helped me see that the key to this lesson was right there, within me. You know, I bet there are all kinds of other considerate mannerisms people possess; I sense there are a lot of class acts out there. I can learn so much from others who have strong people skills. It's amazing how such seemingly small things have such a huge impact on who I am becoming as I grow. I think I also learned today that I respect Jennifer more because, initial annoyance aside, she didn't just hand me an answer.

Could it be that I'm starting to figure things out myself, re-entering the world of "normal" and gaining some confidence?

Turning the Tables

• •

I sit waiting for Jennifer to call my name. Ten minutes pass; she's running late. I look around without staring—because yes, I know that would be rude—and steal glimpses. I notice that there's something quite interesting about every single person in the room waiting to see a health-care provider. I find myself hoping they're all okay. Whoa—that's new! By the time my name is called, I realize that I'm not totally losing it having to wait, the way I used to. I am not sitting here with my head down, glaring at the floor all fired up that Jennifer is making me sit for a measly ten minutes! I have managed to fill my thoughts with positive things instead and just enjoy the moment. That's cool. Very cool.

"So, how was your week?" Jennifer inquires as I enter her office, smiling.

"Excellent. How was yours?"

"Thanks for asking, Heather." I know she noticed that I applied exactly what she told me to do with others, but that's all right. I don't care. I want her to know that I am learning; that's what I'm here for.

"I had a great week," Jennifer reveals. "This weekend, I went up north with my two precious little ones."

This is the first time Jennifer has ever shared anything personal with me, so I'm intrigued. "And what did you do up north?"

"I took them skiing. It was so cute!" She glows, laughing at the memory. "I can ski with my two-year-old between my knees! There's this new device that attaches us to each other."

My heart is warming, a good feeling that I'm not yet used to. I feel "a part" of life instead of "apart" from life. I'm not sure how else to describe it but it lifts me up and I feel connected. I can really imagine how Jennifer must feel skiing down the hill with her toddler. It reminds me again how rewarding relationships are. I used to listen to others but never truly felt or reflected about what they were saying to me. It basically went in one ear and out the other. Taking that extra step to absorb and appreciate what the other person is saying is amazing, and it definitely leads to deeper conversations.

"That is so cute!" I gush—and I mean it!

"Yes, it is really cute." We chat a bit more, then get down to business. "Sooo," Jennifer circles back with sincere interest, as always, "how did your week go?"

"Well, I finally had a chance to go out with my dad one-on-one, and I did exactly what you told me to. He was waiting for me at the table when I got there. I sat down and he said hello, as usual. But did I have a surprise for him! I said hello back then launched right into asking how his day was. And do you know what he did?"

"No, what?" Jennifer is eager to hear.

"He chuckled and said that he can see that you've trained me very well. Busted!" I laughed. "Nothing gets past my dad; he's pretty clever! Obviously he thought that a question about him and his life was a little out of character for me!"

"Ya think?" Jennifer asks sarcastically, which causes us both to giggle. It feels so good to not just notice my weaknesses and work on them, but to be at a point where I can actually laugh about some of my foibles and former ways. Thumbs up!

"That's great, Heather. I would rate that very high on the 'not-so-narcissistic' learning scale." I smile; Jennifer knows I can handle some teasing at this point. "Now, what about the name-dropping concerns you had?"

"Well, I noticed that whenever I talk to this one boss of mine, I start rambling and name-dropping. Maybe he makes me nervous? I totally know that this is a part of me that he doesn't respond well to. He is more task-oriented."

"Well, this is where you can improve your people skills, Heather. Every individual is unique, and so you have to engage each individual in your life differently."

I prove that myself as I respond, "That's so true! Because I also know that if I tell another boss a funny story about my weekend, even if it involves naming names, he is genuinely interested and loves to hear it."

"We are right on track here, Heather. What you've learned is that each circumstance is different, every person is different, and you have to trust your gut and adapt."

My gut, my gut, I repeat in my head like a mantra. I have to start trusting my gut. And you know what? I always kind of thought it was telling me something. Yes, something beyond, "Enough apple pie already!"

No He-mail

. . . .

"So how's it going with your new boyfriend, Heather? It's been what, about six weeks now?"

"Yep. And I'm thinking it's been about two weeks too long! He's not as wonderful as I had originally thought."

"Well, it takes some time before people show their true colours," Jennifer declares.

"Quite honestly, the first four weeks were great, but the past two have been not-so-great."

"And why is that?" she pries, concerned.

"First of all, I've lost a lot of respect for him because I've caught him telling a few white lies."

"Lies are not good, Heather, no matter how white they are. As you are learning, the truth will always find you."

"I know. And sometimes I worry that he's taking advantage of me. I seem to pay for most things, like dinners out. I just feel like he kind of expects me to pick up all the tabs. He pulls the whole going-to-the-washroom-when-the-bill's-about-to-come thing. But here's the worst: He told me he has no fashion sense—and trust me, that is an understatement—so I told him that I would take him shopping for some new clothes."

"Shopping. Well, you would love that! So how was the shopping excursion?"

"Ha! Well, when we got to the counter with a few golf shirts, he just stood there expecting me to pay for them!"

"Seriously?"

"Dead serious."

"Oooh. That does seem a bit unusual."

"I guess he has no pride—another reason I've lost respect for him." Could I perhaps be forming my own opinion for once?

"What did you do about the golf shirts?"

"I paid for them and afterwards, we argued about it. He said, since it was my idea to help him shop, I should be the one to pay for it. And you know that I never argue. I'll do almost anything to avoid it."

"But here's the thing. In a relationship, you should be able to have disagreements."

"Really?"

"Yes. It's healthy to let out your true opinions and emotions."

"I hate conflict," I demur.

"Conflict doesn't necessarily mean that you are screaming and fighting. It simply means that you see things differently and you need to discuss it to understand one another. When couples don't talk about things and stifle their emotions, they end up being resentful, angry and withdrawn."

"Well, when we discussed the shopping trip later, he wouldn't budge. On the up side," I quip, "the shirts do look good on him."

Jennifer smiles. "So, do you like this guy?"

"He's cute and a good golfer, but he never pays or even says thank you. He also never opens the door for me or does polite things like that. And as I already said, he lies. He's just not much of a gentleman."

"The fact that he's a good golfer is not a good reason to date him. You clearly have no respect for him and he is not treating you the way you want to be treated. So why are you still dating him?"

Ohhh, this is embarrassing. "Because it's nice to have a boyfriend," I admit, blushing.

"It's better to be on your own than with someone who is not good for you. You need to listen to your gut, remember? If you're having these kinds of feelings this early in your relationship, it's bound to get worse."

Oh, great. "Really?"

"Usually at this stage of a relationship you're still putting your best foot forward, trying to romance or impress your date."

It's been a while. I had forgotten that. "So what do I do now?" I wonder aloud.

"What do you think?" Jennifer tosses it right back to me.

"I guess I should tell him it's over."

"It sounds like it to me. Perhaps you should meet with him as soon as possible so that you don't lead him on. Just tell him the truth; you want to go your own way."

"Oh dear, Jennifer, I don't know if I can say that! Can't I just email him instead?"

She arches her eyebrows and doesn't hesitate for a second. "Definitely not, Heather. Emails are for making dates and arranging times for things, not for discussing emotions. They get misconstrued. After six weeks, you owe it to him and to yourself to meet in person. Trust me, you will feel better about yourself after you do."

Jennifer has been right so far, so as much as I want to dash off a sayonara email, I call the guy up after my appointment, meet with him and tell him that it's over. To my surprise, he is baffled. His confused response is, "I don't understand why. Tell me what I need to do differently!"

Wow. Echoes of my former self-absorbed, insecure self? I walk away sure that I have made the right decision.

The Truth is Foolproof

● ●

I'm talking to my girlfriend Leanne. For three weeks, she has been dating a new guy she really likes. She's a bit concerned, though, that he gets upset with her whenever she goes out with her friends. Before she met him, she had agreed to go to a corporate Christmas party with another friend who happens to be male. The festivities are in a few days.

Leanne confides, "I told Mike that I was going to my staff Christmas party with one of my girlfriends."

Uh-oh. Lying doesn't work; it just gets you into trouble. "Why didn't you just tell your new boyfriend the truth—that you had committed to going to this party with a guy-pal before he came into the picture?"

She shakes her head. "He gets mad at me even if I just go out with my girlfriends, so if I tell him the truth, it would probably ruin our relationship."

I think about this. Leanne could be right. It might ruin her relationship, but I'm a big believer in telling the truth. Deceit just messes people up. Tangled webs and all that. But I go along with her. "Oh dear, Leanne. It seems like he isn't giving you a choice here. You have to lie in order to keep him."

Yes, I know that lying is wrong. I know that with every fibre of my being. I've found myself in similar situations with my doctor. He likes to say, "You are only as sick as your secrets." He tells me I haven't "recovered" if I eat any diet products. I do, rarely… well, maybe from time to time… almost never, actually, have the occasional spoonful of diet chocolate pudding. Even though I'm healthy, if I told him about this, he would worry and we'd argue, needlessly. By telling the truth, I risk being scolded. It's such a paradox.

I wish I could figure out a solution for Leanne with her boyfriend and for me with my doctors. I know all too well from my ex-boyfriend, "Pinocchio", that when you lie, you usually get caught, and the lying makes everything worse than it would have been. I need to take this to Jennifer. I'm dying to know what she will suggest.

"Heather," she replies after I brief her on our dual dilemmas, "people forget their lies, but they never forget the truth. Furthermore, you and Leanne are not being 'forced' to lie, in either of your cases."

I'm stunned; she has an answer yet again! She seemed entirely confident in her response. "Well, I'm dying to know how, Jennifer, because I've thought it through and I have no idea how Leanne can tell her jealous boyfriend about her male friend, or how I can tell my doctors about my odd mouthful of diet food."

"You both have to preface the truth."

"Preface it?" What the heck is she talking about? I'm not planning on writing a book about my pudding denial.

"Yes, you have to preface it. In Leanne's situation, for instance, she needs to say to her boyfriend, 'I need to tell you something, but I'm concerned that you're going to be upset with me. Our relationship is important to me, but it will only work if I can be completely honest with you.' And then she can say that before she met him, she was invited to this Christmas party by a friend who is a guy. It might actually improve her relationship. It would definitely let Leanne be at peace not having to cover up and lie, and it might make her boyfriend wonder about his own behaviour and why Leanne thought he would be upset."

"Sweet." I give it the stamp of approval. "I like it."

"And you could do it in your situation too, Heather. All you have to do is say to any doctor that you are really afraid of his reaction and concerned he will get upset if you tell him the truth."

"I can picture what that reaction will be," I shudder. "I don't even want to go there."

"That's up to you, but I'm sure any doctor would understand."

The next day I see Leanne and I'm really pumped about giving her the solution to her possessive-boyfriend problem. I blurt out enthusiastically, "Leanne, you just have to preface it and tell him that you're concerned about his reaction but you really want it to work with him. And then tell him you were invited to a Christmas party by a friend who is a guy before you started dating him and you want to honour your commitment. Emphasize the 'before we started dating' part," I add excitedly.

Leanne laughs. It turns out he and she have just had a "somewhat unpleasant," as she puts it, break-up. She giggles, "You know what? I think I should just call him and say, 'By the way, that girlfriend I'm going to the Christmas party with tomorrow night? She is actually a he!'"

I'm still figuring out how to tell the truth to my doctor—or how to keep this book away from him.

Don't Baby Bad Friendships

• •

I am spending a lot of time with a girl who is fun to socialize with but she reminds me of myself in my "pre-recovery life," when it was all about me and if I didn't get my way, watch out. I would persist and persist without thinking of others.

It's Sunday morning and though it's dreary out, I'm happy to have the day to myself to run some errands and watch Intervention, a show that makes me feel like I may be a smidgen more together than I think. I get an email from the girl in question: "Will you come with me to watch the baseball tournament today?" She likes a guy who is playing and needs someone to go with, so she's asking me because I usually bend over backwards to do what she wants.

"No, thanks. It's cold and rainy out and I'm really looking forward to doing my own thing today," I reply.

I am then bombarded with emails from her trying to convince me to go. It's hard for me, but I stand up for myself and type: "I'm really sorry, but I don't want to go in this weather. I have a lot of things I need to get done." She snaps at me via BlackBerry and I end up spending a large part of my day emailing or BBM'ing her and feeling lousy that I let her down. Yeesh; I should have just gone to the baseball tournament. My day couldn't have been any worse or less productive.

"Jennifer," I conclude in my next session, "I feel like a slave to her."

"Why are you friends with her?" Jennifer asks.

I don't have an immediate answer. I'm stumped. So I hit the pause button and take a few minutes to figure it out. I'm not proud of my answer—it's terrible—but it's the truth. "Because I need good friends," I confess.

"Heather, you're using her just as much as she's using you. Can't you see that?"

"Yes, I can," I agree. In that instant, I realize that not all that long ago, I would have become defensive and not admitted to my shortcomings. It feels so good to let the real truth sink in and to let my guard down. In a weird way, I'm really enjoying this choppy voyage of self-discovery. It feels good to say, "Jennifer, what should I do about it? I don't want to be like this."

"This sounds like an unhealthy friendship. What do you think?"

My heart sinks a bit. "But I need her, Jennifer. We do have a lot of good times together. She is my friend."

"This is entirely your choice, Heather. You have to decide if the friendship is meaningful, and if it is, whether you can accept her as she is."

"Maybe she will change," I hazard, trying to figure out how to keep her.

"That's possible. But right now, you know this is who she is and you cannot change her. Are you willing to have your friendship continue like this?" she repeats.

"No. She drains me."

"Then?"

I know Jennifer is right but I wish I could have a healthy relationship with my taxing friend. "How do I do this?" I sigh. "Do I approach her and tell her this?"

"No, there is no need to do that. Put yourself in her shoes. Coming straight out and confronting her might hurt her feelings. Instead you can just slow down with the emails and when she asks you to do something, tell her that you have a lot on your plate right now, which is true. Gradually, the friendship will wind down."

"Okay, Jennifer, I believe you."

The following week, I get an invitation to a baby shower my friend is throwing for a woman I don't know well. The day of the shower, I am booked for a tennis tournament out of town. Perfect timing! I RSVP a thanks and indicate that I can't make it that day. Done... or maybe not. Nothing is ever simple with this girl.

A day later she calls me up. "I am so sorry to hear you can't make it to the baby shower," she says drily.

"Yes, it's a drag but I'm away that day."

"Can't you reschedule?"

"The tennis tournament? No."

"Do you have to play?"

"I would like to. I've been practising for it for the past month."

"Fine."

I hear the distance in her voice before she hangs up the phone. Ouch!

Next, I get this email that totally floors me: "I thought that since this shower is for a mutual friend of ours and being held in my home, you would come and support me and her. It's her first baby. And I don't often throw parties."

It is sooo clear to me now that this is not a true friendship. Jennifer is right; this demanding guilt-inducer is not going to change. She stops speaking to me. This does not feel good, but the next week when I relay the drama to Jennifer, she giggles, "And what did I tell you?"

"That I cannot change others."

"You got it!"

Getting into the Swing of Things

• •

It's a glorious, sunny day. Perfect golf weather. One of the regulars in my foursome can't make it, though, so she's sent a pal of hers to sub. The three of us don't know her sub but we're happy to tee off.

After just two holes of her non-stop chatter, though, we know her all too well. And we are "teed-off." She's telling us all sorts of intimate details about her divorce. She is prattling on and on. I'm thinking it is so strange to be confiding in people you don't even know during a casual round of golf! Around the fourth hole, she decides we should be aware of the diarrhea her daughter had this morning. Too Much Information alert! By the sixth hole, we're aware of every tiny cramp or PMS headache she or her daughter has ever experienced. Oh, and did I mention bloating?

Now I'm getting a little perturbed. Her verbal diarrhea

is spoiling the round for the rest of us. Who talks while other people are swinging or putting, anyway?

After the game, I call the regular in our foursome and jokingly complain about this "Chatty Cathy" she has inflicted on us. Bad news: The non-stop talker is already booked to sub in again tomorrow. *Arrrggh…* Still, I know my friend will have a word with her and ask her to act more appropriately.

However, whatever she told her sub must have gone in one ear and out the other as our second round of golf with her is as annoying as our first. She stays true to form and continues to tell us her life story. Now I am really wound up. I pick up my cell phone, call our usual fourth, and cause a fuss.

"She's doing it again," I hiss into the phone as I angrily stride down the fairway. However, this time our regular seems irritated by me. She says the other two haven't mentioned anything, and oh, by the way, she has to bow out for the next few weeks, so I might as well "get used" to her friend.

Now my regular golfing buddy is annoyed with me, and it's clear over the next few rounds that the new girl is too, as she obviously knows that I groused about her. I have two people upset with me, which is not pleasant. (And on a golf course that could be dangerous!) How did this happen? Jennifer, help!

That Monday, I fill her in on my dilemma.

"Heather," she says, "first, you tried to deal with the

situation indirectly by going to the friend this woman is subbing for. How about speaking directly and politely to the sub herself? You could preface it that you don't want to upset her, but then express your need for quiet so you can concentrate on your game.

"The second point is that you need to deal effectively with your own frustrations, not let them fester. You built up to a breaking point that caused you to act hastily and unwisely when you lashed out at your friend on the phone from the fairway."

Ouch. I sit across from Jennifer, fighting back the tears, because for the first time I can see that I am the root of the problem here. I remain silent and pretend to inspect my fingernails.

"Heather, is there anyone else who would have eventually complained about her?"

"Yes." I know the other two women were getting annoyed; they had said so.

"Then inaction would have been your best action. Perhaps you could have taken the high road, not complained and let the situation handle itself."

"Are you saying I shouldn't have done anything, even though I couldn't golf well while she was burbling and babbling on?"

"That is a judgement call. But don't let anger or frustration drive your decision making. Next time, don't let it fester or act on it impulsively. Instead, stop, breathe and proceed with full awareness. This was not about your golf sub; it was about your tolerance level for agitation. Everyone's is different. In this situation, you could focus on calming yourself and regulating your own emotions. While you are doing that, you are being the bigger person."

Sounds like a first-class approach, getting in the swing of things instead of wanting to swing at things! I'm going to add this to my repertoire.

There for a Reason

I arrive at Jennifer's on cloud nine. I can't wait to broadcast my latest news; I know she's going to love this! We go into her office and she asks, "So, what do we have on our agenda today?"

No "Hello, how are you?" That's fine with me. I can't wait to cut to the chase.

"Jennifer, I'm so thrilled!" I exclaim. "While I was at the golf club this week, I ran into a really cute guy and talked to him. He was there on his own—all tall, blond and handsome. We made small talk about where we went to high school, how old we are and where we work. Then we had to go our separate ways. When I arrived at work on Tuesday, there was an email from him! It said: 'Hey Heather, I'm not cyber-stalking you but I thought you were cute so I looked up your company and found your email. Would you like to go out sometime?'"

"Annnnnd?" Jennifer eggs me on, eagerly.

"I sent him back an email right away saying sure, I'd love to!"

"And then?"

"We went out on Thursday for dinner and it was awesome!" I can tell that Jennifer is excited for me. There is a pause, though, and I know she is going to share something deep. Go figure.

"Heather, you know, every person in your life is there for a reason. When he emailed you, that gave you the confidence you needed in yourself at the time. Whatever happens with this guy, he gave you the positive feedback that you are worthy of getting to know."

I think for a minute—Jennifer never fails to make me stop and think further—and yep, he did make me feel good! Life is on track for the first time in years and I am going to be present and relish this moment, enjoying the Here and Now. If it doesn't happen with this guy, it doesn't matter. He made me feel good about myself and reminded me that today is where life is lived and it's a lot more fun and far more productive than worrying about yesterday or tomorrow.

Berry-itis

I grew up way back when we used a telephone to communicate. Boy, times have changed! Welcome to the world of texting, the cause of a gazillion emotional misunderstandings. If you could hear each other's tone or see their expression, you might have a very different interpretation of a situation. Don't get me wrong: I love texting and I'm as addicted to my BlackBerry as the next person is, but I do know I could use it (or not use it) more wisely.

My bladder wakes me up in the middle of the night. I zombie-walk to the bathroom and stumble back into bed. There's my BlackBerry, winking at me in the dark. I'm half asleep but feel compelled to check it. I press the trackball, which lights up with two new messages. Yesss! Somebody loves me! Gotta check 'em, check 'em now. Oh, the disappointment: one is spam, the other a mass email invitation to a Superbowl party. I hurl my head back onto my pillow, but I don't fall back asleep, because now I'm thinking about the party.

The next day I'm tired and if I'm tired I am grumpy and can't deal with anything. I just feel out of sorts. I learned this lesson years ago when I had to work over-time during tax season and I burst into tears in front of my supervisor. (Usually, it's the tax filers bursting into tears, not the tax accountants!) When I told a friend about that incident, she asked if I had been tired.

"I was exhausted!"

"Nothing is right when you are tired," she commiser-ated. "I can cry at the drop of a hat when I'm tired. Things get magnified and bother us way more when we're sleep deprived. Then we get some rest and we all feel better in the morning."

I will never forget those words. She was right. (As a sidebar, this friend was just as right as she was when she told me that hiring a cleaning lady was the best money I would ever spend.)

Anyway, this morning when I begrudgingly decide to stop staring at the bedroom ceiling, the first thing I do is grab my BlackBerry. I have five new messages! Awe-some! It's five people replying to the party invitation. I read them all.

I get to work and put my Berry beside my keyboard. It vibrates with another reply to the party. When I pick it up, I feel compelled to text the guy I went out with last week: "Good morning, Adam. How was your weekend?"

Every ten minutes, I'm checking to see if Adam has

responded. Nothing. Nothing. Nothing. And yet more nothing. My spirits are sinking further. My BlackBerry vibrates again; this time it's a girlfriend on Messenger. I read it and then remember that on Messenger, she can tell I have read it. She's asking what my plans are for tonight. I'm not sure yet because it depends how I feel after work, so I don't really know. I don't want to respond to this right now but because she can tell that I have read it, she will think I am rude if don't. There is a whole pressure-filled social etiquette to BlackBerrying. I feel distracted and unproductive. I've now used up twenty minutes of my day checking for messages. I respond to my friend: "Not sure yet."

There. Finally, I can focus on work. Or can I? The BlackBerry vibrates… could it be Adam replying to my message? Damn; it's my girlfriend again asking me to commit to a 5:15 tee time. Possibly, but I just want to play it by ear. Still, it feels like it would be rude to say no, so I say yes.

A colleague at work snaps, "Heather, can you please take your BlackBerry off vibrate? That noise is driving me nuts."

I feel terrible. "Of course."

Good. Saved from myself.

Well, that lasts about two seconds, then every five minutes I start clicking the ball track (quietly!) to see if Adam has responded to my message. No response. Still no response. Yet again no response… Argggh. This is emotionally draining. Oh, now I see that my girlfriend hasn't opened my Messenger message about golf tonight—is she ignoring me, too? How dare she! My heart sinks again. It's already 10 a.m. and I have yet to start my work.

No wonder this addictive little gizmo is nicknamed CrackBerry. If ever you had insecurity issues, they are definitely going to be triggered by this blasted machine! Clearly, I'm still working through my insecurities. I can hear Jennifer's voice in my head. "Heather, why don't you try to temper your use of the BlackBerry? Perhaps you could set aside a few times each day when you will allow yourself to check it. In addition, you can set your boundaries with others by leaving a voicemail or automatic message indicating when you are checking in."

Excellent, sound advice. Brilliant. I will definitely do this! It makes so much sense. I'll do it, just as soon as I check for Adam just a few more times... And am I on for 5:15 golf? Will my girlfriend ever open my message? And wait, is that another response to the Superbowl invitation...

Excel-ling at Work

● ●

I'm working on an important file that my boss wants done ASAP. It's Friday afternoon and he asks me when he can expect to see it. I know I still have a lot of work to do but I feel pressured by this question so I tell him what I think he'd like to hear.

"I will have it on your desk by Monday morning," I respond, trying to be a respectful employee.

He is visibly pleased. "Great!"

I have now committed to spending my entire weekend doing accounting. Oh joy, oh bliss.

After working on it all day Saturday and Sunday, I realize that there is a lot of missing information and I cannot meet my Monday commitment. I'm stressed and troubled; I sincerely want to be a dependable employee, but I see that I have given myself an impossible deadline in order to satisfy my boss. That was short-sighted.

After over two years of my goof-ups, I have yet to stump Jennifer. I'm counting on her counsel so that I never have to relive this situation.

The only hitch is that I have to show up for work tomorrow before my appointment with Jennifer and tell my boss that I did not make my deadline. I decide to apply one of my favourite approaches: prefacing. This should do Jennifer proud.

I get out of my car at work on Monday morning and guess who is pulling up beside me? Who else but my boss! We get out of our cars and I immediately launch into prefacing the bad news. I don't want to wait until he asks me, because I need to ensure he sees me as being responsible.

"Good morning," I say with a smile. "I want to update you on that job. I really don't want to disappoint you because I realize how important it is for me to finish it. But I was not able to complete it for today's deadline due to missing information. I'm really sorry. I didn't anticipate that and I feel terrible."

I'm holding my breath. Did it work?

"All right. We can give the client what we have so far and tell him what we need."

Phew. I can see that he is not overly thrilled, but he's also not angry and he seems to have appreciated my direct approach. Yo, baby! I share the story of my ambitious over-commitment with a co-worker and she says she can't wait to hear what solution Jennifer has in store.

That afternoon, I relay the tale to Jennifer. "I don't want to put myself in this situation again, so what should

I have said? I just feel so pressured when my boss asks me when something will be done."

"This is a great question. You don't have to feel like you have a crystal ball, Heather. The last time I looked, you were human!" We laugh. "Often you can rely on your boss to give you some direction, so you can turn it back to him by asking, 'When are you hoping it will be done?' or 'When are you expecting it?' Put the ball back in his court. Let him give you a clear picture of the expectations."

Sounds like a bit of a tennis rally to me so I should be able to do it. "That could work, but what if he gives me an unrealistic deadline?"

"What do you think, Heather?"

"I don't know," I grin. "You tell me."

She sighs, good-naturedly. "Heather, asking for reassurance from me will only last you about half an hour and get you nowhere. Think for a minute and tell me what you should do."

I mull it over and say, "I guess I'd revert to my number one life rule: Honesty is the best policy."

"Excellent!" Jennifer exclaims. She knows that in the past, I would have sabotaged myself by trying too hard to please, taking on something even if I sensed it might be "Mission Impossible" and not considering other options. Jennifer continues, "You can give your boss your projected timeline, but keep in mind that it is always important to build in a bit of flex time, because we can never fully anticipate every little detail. Projects are often bigger than we originally think. When you give yourself some flex time, you decrease your own stress level."

"Got it. I can do that," I say with confidence.

"I have another suggestion for you, Heather. Develop a system to keep track of your workload and due dates. Perhaps like this." She rifles through some papers and hands me an example of what she does, methodically and in a very orderly fashion, on an Excel spreadsheet; just what I like.

"You could involve your bosses by telling them that you will be updating your spreadsheet weekly to keep both them and yourself informed and up to date. This will demonstrate that you are taking responsibility and they'll appreciate your professionalism."

"Yes, they will."

I go back to the office and my co-worker wants to know what Jennifer's solution was.

"It was to create a tracking sheet like this, to hand in to the partners once a week to keep both them and myself up to date." I show her the nicely set-up spreadsheet.

"Oh no, Heather," she says, wagging her finger, teasingly. "Now they're going to make all of us do this!"

Another co-worker who can overhear the conversation pipes up, "What are you going to do once a week?"

My friend sarcastically answers for me, with a roll of her eyes, "She's going to make a time-tracking sheet just like this every week, so the partners can see how hard she's working." She holds the spreadsheet aloft as evidence.

"Oh man, Heather, kiss up, why don't you!" We all laugh.

It feels good to be organized and to show that I care, because I genuinely do. I feel self-assured and far more in control of my time. This should really help me "Excel" at work.

Home Alone

• •

"Good morning," my tennis partner croaks at an obscenely early hour on Monday morning at the club.

"Hey, you look tired. What were you up to this weekend?" I have to ask her.

"Oh, Heather, I had the best time Saturday night. I went to a party and got home at some ridiculous hour of the morning. I'm still recovering!" We giggle. "What did you do Saturday night?"

I'm a bit embarrassed to tell her that I spent Saturday night at home alone. "Well, I stayed in, baked my favourite chocolate chip cookies—I've had a craving—and watched American Idol that I PVR'ed. I was in bed by nine! That was what I wanted to do and I really enjoyed it. I'm such a nerd!"

"Sounds like a good night to me, Heather. After this weekend, I'm looking forward to spending next Saturday night just chillin' at home, too. I love a free night to myself," she adds with conviction.

"You do?" I always thought that made me a bore, so I'm puzzled.

"Absolutely! Everyone needs time to wind down once in a while."

"So I'm not a nerd after all?"

"Nope, you took care of yourself. What is nerdy is what you did the weekend before, when you spent forty-eight hours doing accounting! Now that, that's nerdy!"

"Thanks for the pep-talk," I smile. That was definitely a morale booster. As we head to the courts, she's slowly waking up and I'm no longer ashamed to have spent a Saturday night just chillin' by myself. I knew it was for self-care, I feel validated, and I'm pretty sure in her state, I'm going to win this game!

R-E-S-P-E-C-T

• •

I'm at the golf course, watching the final round of the Canadian Juniors tournament with a friend. When it ends, she has to go but I want to stay around and savour this glorious summer day. I look over at the patio and notice my dad sitting with three other men. Hmm… I probably shouldn't sit with them because I'll feel like I'm intruding on "the boys" and I don't think he would appreciate that. But I do want to stay, so reluctantly I walk over to his table and try a new approach.

"Hello, Dad. I was just wondering if you mind if I join you and your friends for a bit?"

"Sure," he says, welcoming me. My heart fills. Amazing. In the past, I would have moseyed on over, plunked myself down and not been welcome. This simple act of asking for permission first feels wonderful. My dad's warm response feels even better. Showing him the respect he deserves makes him respect me back. It's magic. Now I can just sit here, listen as a guest and enjoy this splendid summer day, just like I wanted to.

I repeat this story to Jennifer, who paraphrases my learning: "What you give out, you get back."

Now I give everyone my respect because it feels great to be respected back and I now know that I, too, deserve that feeling. A little thought before proceeding sure goes a long way.

The wonderful by-product of respecting others is that they will respect you in return, which bolsters our own self-esteem. I never knew how important this approach really was until I experienced it in my own life with the three partners I work for at my accounting firm. I have learned that there are no hard-and-fast rules about how to treat bosses because, like all of us, each one is an individual. (Newsflash: Bosses are human!) We have to modify our behaviour to adapt to each person in our lives.

I have a boss, a nice guy, who I tried to treat as more of a friend. However, whenever I told him anything about my personal life, he shut me out and I would feel disrespected. Then I learned the boundary that I need to keep between this particular individual and myself. He prefers to keep office interactions strictly professional. When I stopped sharing my personal life, he started responding to me far more favourably. This new-found understanding and respect showed themselves within a few short weeks of me changing my behaviour. Once I showed him the respect and distance he deserved and preferred as a boss, I received the respect that I wanted back. It was almost instantaneous. I was awe-struck and felt fulfilled.

But as I said, the same behaviours don't hold true for everyone. I have another boss who's just the opposite: He loves to hear my personal stories. He enjoys my anec-dotes and finds humour in my "Lucy"-like antics. He wants to hear how I did at golf or tennis and about the parties I've been to on the weekend. So as I said, we have to gauge and treat each person on an individual basis. Trust your instincts and learn from your mistakes. Keep doing what works and stop doing what doesn't.

I now have a wonderful relationship with all of my bosses and they are all very different, caring people. I feel great going to work every day knowing how to behave with each of them, and feeling comfortable with all of them.

Timeless Classics

● ●

I walk into the locker room at the gym. A friend of mine is putting on her workout clothes while munching on a chocolate chip cookie the size of her head.

"Hi, Heather," she mumbles.

"Hi, Catherine. You going for a workout?"

"Yeah," she laughs, "and the last thing I need right before my workout is this huge cookie! But they make the best chocolate chip cookies here—probably to keep you here longer, working them off! How's your book coming, anyway?"

"Thanks for asking," I reply. "Actually, I wrote an entry last night."

"About what?"

"About respect, and how if you give it out, you get it back."

"That's so true. It's one of those little things in life that is so important."

She is looking me in the eye. She's confident, animated,

definitely in the moment, asking me questions and interested in my answers.

"Catherine, this is funny because right now you are doing a lot of the things that I talk about in my book!"

"Like what?"

"Like being interested in others and being in the present moment and looking me in the eye."

"Good, because those are things that I know are really important but not taught enough. They can't be over-emphasized."

"Yeah, kind of like calling people by name. My parents always taught me to say, 'Hello Mr. or Mrs. So-and-So,' and boy does it ever make the conversation more personal. It's such a small thing that makes such a big difference."

"Yeah, I always look people in the eye and call them by name—if I remember their name that is," she giggles. "Now you've got me thinking about the simple things that are really important that I learned when I was young. My parents also taught me that when they introduce me to someone, I should give them a firm, solid handshake, not offer my hand like a limp, dead fish!"

"Eww, I hate when people do that. You've gotta squeeze it a bit to show a bit of confidence."

By now we are upstairs ready to do our respective workouts. I smile at Catherine, who turns to look me in the eye again. She says, "I can't wait to read it, Heather. People don't tend to talk about this stuff. Sometimes respect, etiquette and courtesy seem like things from a bygone era."

"Awww... thanks, Catherine."

That conversation really reinforces that these seemingly minor habits are key to classic people skills. Catherine seems to be quite polished at them all. No wonder everyone says what a nice person she is. She is one smart cookie.

The Hamburglar

● ●

I am going out for dinner with a good friend tonight and I'm looking forward to an evening of camaraderie. I love the fact that I am genuinely having fun socializing, and feeling like the "real" me again. I feel so "normal"—if there even is a normal! I look at the menu. Eight-ounce classic sirloin burger with fries. I salivate just thinking about it; I haven't had red meat in so long. Mmm, I can taste it. I want it. I want it bad. A juicy burger, maybe dribbling just a bit down my chin... I bet it comes with fries... Do they have gravy? I wonder. The waitress arrives.

"Grilled chicken sandwich with a side salad, please." Who said that?

Wait, I did. I've eaten enough today, darn it. The hamburger has too many calories and I don't want to see the scale two pounds heavier tomorrow. Part of me realizes this is limiting me but at the moment, I'm certain I'm making the right choice.

I eat the grilled chicken burger, which doesn't even taste good. I'm not satisfied at all. My friend, on the other hand, ordered the entree she really wanted and has only eaten about half of it! What's up with that? She offers some to me and it's mmm-mmm good. We end up talking and laughing and all the while, I am gorging on the rest of my friend's meal. At one point, when she makes a sudden move toward her plate, I slap her hand.

We go to the movies. I feel full but not satisfied. Well, well, what have we here? The snack bar! I pause. I hear the siren song of popcorn popping. I move in. The next thing I know, I have procured a bag of chocolate-covered almonds. And not just any bag, either; a gigantic, movie-size bag!

"I'll just have a few," I say to myself. Apparently I meant a few fistfuls, because by the end of the movie, the mega-pack is empty. Good Lord, I don't even know what the movie was about because all through it I've been battling my inner demons, swearing that each almond will be my last.

As I drive home, trying not to glance at any drive-thrus, I realize that tonight, I totally missed the boat. No, not the gravy boat. Had I just ordered the hamburger in the first place and eaten until I was pleasantly full, I would have enjoyed the movie. I would not have obsessed about food and I would not have awakened two pounds heavier the next day—which I did, because I ended up eating so much in compensation.

I didn't trust my instincts or listen to what my body was telling me when it was calling out Burger, Burger, Burger! I guess these internal cues are there for a reason. Lesson learned. Don't ignore them and make decisions impulsively. Next time, I'll slow down and pay attention to my body's desires and say to the waitress, "Hamburger, please, with fries."

Say No to the Yes Man

● ●

I've been seeing Jennifer for a year now and during that time I have re-established my relationships with my tennis, golf and work friends as well as cultivating new ones. I am also still working full-time. I kinda feel like I deserve a gold medal!

My sister Sonja calls me up. "Hey Heather, Eric is on his school holidays this week. I'm wondering if you can teach him some tennis?"

The thought of my nephew brings a bright smile to my face and I instantly agree. "I'd love to. How about we do a half-hour every day on my lunch break?"

"That would be perfect! Thanks a million, Heather."

I'm so glad that I just made my amazing sister happy!

Later on in the day, I get a message on my BlackBerry from my best friend: "I know this is last minute but would you be able to golf after work today? I'm playing with the boys and we want you to join us."

Hooray! It's beautiful beyond my office windows and the greens are beckoning. This must be my lucky day. "For sure," I respond instantly.

I let my plans sink in for a second and realize that I'm going to have to leave work early to go home to grab my golf clothes. I was planning on doing my laundry and grocery shopping tonight but I guess that will have to wait until tomorrow. Wait. Uh-oh. I almost forgot that I'm teaching my nephew tennis at lunch. How am I going to finish this file that's due tomorrow morning?

The next day, I wake up extra early for work so I can have that file on my boss's desk at 9 a.m. I'm stressed and tired, but I did have fun last night. I'm already looking forward to this evening, when I'll be able to go home and unwind. As visions of jammies and bathrobes dance in my head, my phone rings and a girlfriend cheerily asks, "Hey, would you like to go out for dinner tomorrow? We haven't seen each other in a long time."

I'm pooped out and know it but don't want to disappoint my friend (plus I'm dying for that hamburger). "Sure, that would be perfect!" I reply cheerily, in reality preferring to do it in a few days because I need a breather.

That night I forget all about my laundry, go to bed early, wake up feeling better, and realize to my horror that I have no clean clothes to wear to work. Tonight I'm going out for dinner so I won't have any clean clothes for tomorrow, either! I feel rushed, unsettled and anxious—feelings I loathe. Where is that calm and relaxed state of mind that I worked so hard for and love so much? Maybe Jennifer will know.

In the meantime, I cancel dinner with my girlfriend in order to un-busy myself. I hate cancelling, though. I feel conscience-stricken and I don't want a reputation for being unreliable.

How do I get rid of this guilt? I hope Jennifer knows.

I turn my questions over to her at our next appointment and, as always, she provides me with optimal solutions.

"Why do you continually say yes to everything, Heather?" she challenges me.

"Well, this time I wanted to make Sonja happy by teaching Eric; plus it's nice to see them."

"Instead of committing yourself at lunchtime every day, could you have taught him one or two days instead? Perhaps you wouldn't have been so overwhelmed with work piling up and it still would have made both you and Sonja happy. It doesn't have to be all or nothing, Heather."

"Hindsight is 20/20," I agree. "Now, I said yes to the golf because I didn't want to miss out."

"Never do anything because you are afraid of missing out," she advises me. "Be authentic, follow the path of your intuition and do what makes you feel happy and balanced. In this instance, what would that have been?"

"Definitely to golf, I really like those friends, but I just had so much going on. However, had I not promised to play tennis every day, making time for golf wouldn't have been such an issue."

"This is called balance," Jennifer informs me.

"Balance?" I echo, then joke, "That's a new word for me; I better look it up!"

"Yes, you better!" We both smile, then Jennifer gets right back to work. "And the dinner you cancelled on?" she presses.

"I felt awful about cancelling; the guilt distracted me for a big part of the day."

"And do you think your girlfriend would have cared had you asked for a different day?"

"Absolutely not," I realize. "And then I wouldn't have had to cancel and I would have spared myself all that guilt!"

"So what are you going to do the next time someone asks you to do something?"

Oh, dear. I better get this right. "Take more time to think about it? Choose what's best for me without feeling pressured to please others?"

"Exactly. Stop, breathe and proceed with full awareness. Respond, don't react. Learn your limits and respect them. Learn to say 'no' to the 'yes' man."

I mull it over: Say no to the yes man. "Yes, ma'am!" I leave with a plan that I can apply on a daily basis.

Soul Food

• •

I'm so exhausted that I don't particularly want to go and meet Jennifer today. And by now, you know that that means I am pretty exhausted! I also have nothing important to share. Things are going just fine and nothing happened this week that I think I need to discuss.

"You look tired today," Jennifer points out, straight off.

"I'm worn out, Jennifer."

"What happened this week?" she inquires.

"Absolutely nothing. I honestly don't have anything to talk about today."

She looks at me pointedly. Generally, I have such a list of things to discuss that we have a hard time getting through them in an hour.

"How is your sleeping?" she asks with purpose.

"I've been going to bed late because I've been golfing every day after work. Then I end up staying on the patio for dinner and by the time I get home it's late and I have to wake up early for work. So, to answer your question, I guess I haven't been sleeping as much as I usually do."

"And how much time did you spend golfing this week?"

I know she is going somewhere with this. "Every night for four hours," I respond frankly. Wow, that sounds like a lot when I say it out loud!

She continues to probe. "And then you stay for dinner on the patio afterward?"

"Yes," I answer, reluctantly.

"So, did you teach your nephew tennis this week?"

I normally teach him for a half-hour each week and I love it because I get to spend time with him and my sister. "Unfortunately, I didn't have time," I sigh. "I wish I could have. I enjoy that half hour."

"Is this how you want to continue, Heather?"

"Definitely not. I feel so worn-out."

"Well, I think it's time we make your pie of life."

Pie of life? What is she talking about? Might apples and cinnamon be involved? Apparently not. She takes out a piece of paper with two empty circles on it and directs me. "I want you to fill out what percentage of time you spent on specific activities this week in this first empty pie."

"Okay." I have a feeling that I am going to learn something huge today, after all. I just hope I can stay awake for the revelation. I fill out the first empty circle, I can "do the math." I know that I spent eight hours at work every day, four hours golfing and two hours on the patio. I spent six hours sleeping and the rest are unaccounted for. I show her my pie with only the four categories in it.

"And what happened to all of those little things that you enjoy, like spending time with your family, reading, watching American Idol and having some 'me' time?"

"Those things appear to have gone by the wayside."

"Well, no wonder you feel so out of sorts; those are the things that fill you up."

"They do? That doesn't make sense because they are such a small part of my life. If I were to add them to my pie, they would only take about ten percent of it."

"That's a great point, Heather, because what I'm going to make clear to you right now is that without that ten percent, you feel like you do right now—exhausted and empty. You haven't made time for the small but critical things in your life. Now, what is most important to you?"

"My health," I answer in a heartbeat, because I know all too well that without it, I have nothing.

"Okay. What's next?"

"My family and friends."

"And Heather, where are they in the pie you just drew?"

"Nowhere!" I have an aha moment.

"And now do you know why you feel the way you do?"

"I haven't been giving priority to what really matters to me. Instead, I've been filling myself up with less important things."

"There you have it. Now I want you to draw how you would like your pie to look."

In the second circle, I add more time for sleep, tennis with my nephew, friends, reading and of course American Idol. "You know what's remarkable about this, Jennifer?"

"What?"

"The critical things that fill me up and recharge me actually don't take much time at all!"

"Very observant, Heather. Now act on this knowledge and see how you feel in a few days."

"I will."

I feel better already and leave with renewed direction and purpose. Thank goodness I came today or I would have spent another week living aimlessly, feeling hollow and listless, not feeding my soul.

The Right Ingredients

• •

One week later, I feel rejuvenated and like myself again. It's my regular appointment day and I'm on top of everything. Again I wonder if I really need to go, but after last week I realize that with Jennifer, you never know what you might learn.

"You look re-energized today, Heather," Jennifer points out instantly.

"Yep. I feel like myself again. All I needed to do last week was reset my priorities and follow through on them. It's incredible how such a small thing can make all the difference in the world."

"So did you teach your nephew tennis this week?"

"Twice," I beam.

"So you like the pie of life you made last week?"

I smile, "Yes. In fact, it worked so well that I don't know what we are going to talk about today. Everything is smooth sailing."

"Excellent, because now we can focus on something really constructive."

"What is that?" I'm really curious about what she has on our agenda.

"You're going to make another pie. I'll call it your self-esteem pie."

"Oh brother, this sounds weird."

She smiles in a confident manner and then jokingly asks, "Where's your faith?"

I laugh out loud and let her steer the ship.

"How do you want to be and how do you want to be perceived?"

"Athletic, smart, confident, modest, genuine and down to earth," I reply. I think to myself: This pie could be sweet. This might be exciting.

"Okay, then this week how can you act smart, confident, modest, genuine and down to earth and continue with your sports?"

"It sounds easy enough, but there's one big problem: People don't see me as modest and I don't think they'll ever change that opinion of me."

"You just might be pleasantly surprised."

"Really?"

"Really. It takes very little time at all."

"So, Jennifer, when I come to you next week and say I have nothing to talk about, will you have more new tricks up your sleeve?"

"Heather, life is a constant learning process for all of us. As long as you're open minded and willing to learn, the process never ends. The nice thing about you,

Heather, is your desire to be the very best person that you can be. I see that you want to live authentically, do what feels right for you and let that guide you in developing your own values and a strong sense of self. I admire you for that."

I leave thinking that I like the ingredients of the self-esteem pie. I will devote the week to being athletic, smart, confident, modest, genuine and down to earth. I wonder if others will notice, as Jennifer says they will. I wonder if they will notice that I'm trying hard to behave with good taste.

Going Forward, Backwards

• •

After playing tennis at a national level, I know how to pay scrupulous attention to every minute dynamic of the game. This gives me an appreciation while watching or playing other sports when I'm not intimately acquainted with the high level of intricacies involved. I can illustrate this (painfully!) with my golf swing.

When I first started, I would swing the club as if I were playing tennis and to me, things seemed to be going just fine. The ball and I were connecting more often than not. It was staying on the fairway more often than not. Then I took my first lesson. The golf pro watched me take a few swings and said, "Professional golfers swing from the inside out. Heather, you're doing it from the outside in."

I'm doing it backwards? Oh, dear. I practise and practise trying to swing properly but I keep catching myself going back to swinging in reverse. It's so frustrating because I can envision the proper way but I can't execute it. And now I know that not only is my swing not as good as I previously thought it was—it's actually bad. I mean, when I thought fellow golfers were looking at me admiringly, they were probably looking at me in shock and disbelief. Heck, they were probably worried I was going to back over them with my golf cart.

To this day, I still try to get that proper path and when I do nail it, it feels wonderful and the ball soars!

With anything in life, not just sports, the more I know, the more I realize how much more there is to know. My father once said to me, "Life is a constant learning process." Is it ever! I relate this to my work with Jennifer, where the more I learn about what's important in life such as people skills, being in the moment and staying healthy, the more I can see what I need to change or improve in my daily life. I am definitely not perfect at golf—or anything—but more and more, I am determined to go out swinging.

Exuding Competence

● ●

I'm keen to start the work day, but I want to do something short and straightforward so I can ease into it. I open up a file that my boss says should be pretty easy. I soon notice that the client's cash from last year doesn't balance correctly, the inventory figure was not checked properly; the list goes on. Okay, I am not finding it all that clear-cut and it's taking me a long time. When I finally finish, I hand it in and point out to my boss what I have corrected. He thanks me for the work and assures me that next year, it should be easier. Phew; he appreciates my effort and diligence.

Twelve months later, I am put on the same file again. I've recently taken an in-depth tax course, so I'm smarter now and expect it will take me a lot less time to do it. Think again. Now I see tax-planning opportunities and other issues that I didn't know enough to address last year. The file takes me even longer to do. I hand it to my boss and say, "I found some opportunities here that I couldn't see last year so it was actually more complex to do this time."

I hope he's not upset that I took so long. Again.

His feedback stops my marathon worrying. "Great insights, Heather," he remarks as he looks through it. "The client will be pleased to hear about these saving opportunities."

Leaving his office, I turn around and smile. "Isn't it weird that the more we know, the more we see and things actually become more complex instead of easier?"

"It's a bit ironic, isn't it?" he agrees.

"It would be easier to be oblivious!" I remark flippantly.

I realize now that it's better for me to focus on being the professional I want to be and I've discovered that if I am pleased with my work, my boss will likely be as well.

Maybe you can't just exude confidence; maybe you can exude competence, too.

Lies Do Catch Up With You

● ●

"Remember the guy who told the white lies, from about a year ago?" I'm dying to spill this story to Jennifer.

"Yes."

"I didn't mention this to you at the time, but when he left that night, he took two gift certificates that we got at a golf tournament off of my kitchen table."

"Did you see him do it?"

"No. I just know they were there for about a week, and they disappeared the night he left in a tizzy."

"Did you ask him if he took them?"

"Yes, and he denied it."

"So what did you do about it?"

"Nothing, but the funny thing is that I saw him when I was getting coffee this morning."

"And he returned the gift certificates?"

"Ha ha, no, quite the opposite! I told him that I liked the new shirt he was wearing and he said, 'Yeah, I got it a while ago using those gift certificates we got!'"

"No way! What did you say?"

"I said, 'You mean the ones you took off of my kitchen table?' He was stumped for a second and then said, 'Well, no, I got another set.'"

"Oh my gosh!"

"Yeah! And I didn't even bother to pursue it because of course he would cover that lie with another lie!"

"I'm a firm believer in honesty being the best policy," Jennifer sighs. "You never forget the truth, but you run a very high risk of forgetting the lies."

"I know! What's wrong with telling the truth, anyway?"

"Well," Jennifer speculates, "I suppose that sometimes people are afraid of the immediate consequences. People also don't like to look foolish so at times, because of their feelings of guilt or shame, they may cover up something really innocuous. For me, though, it's always a question of integrity."

"I am well aware of that, Jennifer! You have been so honest with me even when you're giving me difficult feedback. In return, I've been brutally honest with you and I know that transparency is why I am doing so well now.

"And I guess I've got to hand it to him," I grin, "he must have learned something from me because he looked pretty good in his new shirt!"

Role Reversal

•••

I've kept in touch with the guy who took me on a date then politely confirmed that all I had talked about was myself. That still stings. I've learned a lot of lessons in Life 101, so when he calls me up to tell me he has left his job and is going away for two months, I agree to see him again to wish him bon voyage over a quick drink. The only day he can meet is Tuesday. It's not the best day for me, but I shuffle my schedule and leave work early in order to be at the restaurant at four.

I walk in right at our designated meeting time. He's not there yet so I take a seat. Ten minutes pass... then fifteen... I'm thinking that I just left work early to meet him and he's not even employed, so that's not very respectful of him. I sit and wait patiently, though, as there is no point in stressing. I know that I cannot influence when he will arrive. Five minutes later, he walks in.

"Hey, Heather, sorry I'm late."

He gives me a hug and I say, "You look great!" And he did look cute in his jeans and white tee-shirt.

"Yes, thanks. I've been working out."

Oh, so he agrees with me! And where is my, "Hey, Heather, you look good, too"? I'm over-analyzing this. Brush it off, Heather.

"Why did you decide to leave the company? You were so good at your job," I comment as we take our seats.

"That's true. Actually, I was the best at it." The best at it? Who says that? I'm becoming a little perturbed by his attitude.

"Yes, you were good," I agree, because I've worked with him and he was. "So what are you going to do now?"

"I'm going to Taiwan for two months to meet a Buddhist teacher that I know. I called him up and he said that I could stay with him for awhile. But get this: When I was talking to him, he told me that while I am there, I have to have total respect for him and call him 'Teacher.'"

"Well," I say, "calling him 'Teacher' would show respect."

"It's going to be really hard for me to do that," the aspiring student confides, "because I have a hard time looking up to anyone."

At this point it's clear that the only person he does look up to is himself. We spend the next forty-five minutes talking about his trip and a girl he has recently started dating who will soon be left behind for two months.

"Isn't it going to be hard to be apart from her for so long when your relationship is so new?" I ask out of genuine concern.

"I don't think it will be; she told me that she'd wait for me. And she and I both know I'm worth the wait." Did I just hear that? He must be kidding, but he's gazing at me earnestly. I inadvertently choke on a sip of my drink.

The waiter comes over. "Would you two like to order some food?"

"Yes," Mr. "Worth the Wait" says without conferring with me. "We just need a few minutes with the menu."

Oh dear, I don't want to stay here any longer than I have to. I want to go and do what I had originally planned: visit my mom and dad tonight. All will not be lost if I can escape. I want to make a graceful exit, but if push comes to shove, I am willing to throw myself through the floor-to-ceiling window behind him.

"Actually, I'm going to go see my parents, so I can't stay," I tell him sadly.

"Oh!" He seems a little shocked. He says to the waiter, "Well, the lady has to go." The lady? I glance around. Oh, he means me! Yikes; do I ever have to go!

As I drive to my parents' place, I wish I hadn't left work early to meet him; he talked about himself the whole time and showed no interest in my life. Well, many, many months ago, before I knew better, I did the same thing to him. Self-absorption is so unattractive.

Then it dawns on me: Hey, I have learned a lot! Yes, having that life lesson reinforced was definitely worth leaving work early for.

Positive Momentum

● ·

Through the course of therapy, I have been directed countless times to think of the many good things in my life. To practise being grateful. To be grateful even for the hard times. Jennifer says that it's through the hard times that we learn about ourselves and grow. Yadda yadda yadda. But I know she's right.

I've been waiting patiently for our appointment for the past fifteen minutes, and I occupy my time thinking of all of the awesome things that I have in my life. I have a great job, my health, a wonderful family, a beautiful home... What more could I ask for? I had heard of this "being grateful" thing for years and thought it was too "out there" to really work. But now that I have done it and really felt it, I totally understand how it works. Fill yourself with positive thoughts and you fill yourself with good feelings. I love good feelings because they—you guessed it—make you feel good! It's a much smarter train of thought than being frustrated that Jennifer is running late. She's probably helping someone, the way she helps me. I can definitely wait, I realize with a smile.

"Heather," Jennifer calls me in. "How are you?" she asks as I take a seat.

"Great! And how are you?"

"I'm great, too, thanks."

I have to giggle. When I see Jennifer's curious look, I explain, "I went out for lunch on Friday with two guy friends and one of them has a life theory that we should always be sure we are having fun and enjoying ourselves. The other guy has the philosophy that if you give out positive, you will get back positive. I agreed with him and then he told us a story. And that's why I'm laughing."

"What was his story, Heather?"

"He said that he knows an older man who says he's great whenever you ask him how he is. So one time my friend said to him, 'You can't be great every single day,' and the old man said, 'I'm not, but if I give out that positive, I get a positive response back and that cheers me up, and I feel a bit better.'"

"Ahh, and we both said we were 'great' today," Jennifer clues in.

"But the best thing about it is that we mean it," I tell her happily. "I'm noticing that now I only like hanging around fun, positive people. Oh, and I went to church on Sunday with two of my friends and heard something similar there, too: Spread positive energy and surround yourself with positive people."

"Heather, it seems like you're really developing a healthy and happy life."

"Who'd've thunk it?" I marvel. "And it hasn't even taken that long!"

"That's because you've really stayed focused on your recovery, Heather." Jennifer is unmistakably and genuinely pleased. "You have wanted this badly, done it for yourself this time, and now you're harvesting the fruits of your labour."

Jennifer reminds me of another lesson I just had reinforced in the same service. "The speaker at church also talked about that exact thing: focus," I say. "He told a story about how he was having a heart-monitor test done and he had to run on the treadmill for it. He was running along just fine until he went to grab for his towel, and then he stumbled and fell off the treadmill. He was really embarrassed in front of the nurses, but he was okay.

"I didn't really know what point he was trying to make, and then he said, 'Guess why I fell? Because I lost my focus on running when I grabbed for my towel.' The lesson here is that you have to stay focused. You can't lose focus for even a split second.

"Boy, could I ever relate to that!" I laugh. "When I consistently focus on what I want, what I need and what's important to me, my life stays on track. You know, Jennifer, I now have a habit that when I wake up every morning, I remind myself of the wonderful people and things in my life and I remind myself to stay focused on what really matters. I get out of bed on the right side, I start each day on the right foot, and I don't concern myself with things I don't want in my life. It's a simple daily check, no exceptions, come rain or shine."

"That's fantastic, Heather."

As I drive home, I realize I'm learning how to keep my life's positive momentum by simply focusing and paying attention to my priorities and my gut. Sheer genius through its sheer simplicity. Oh, and that guy who just cut in front of me without signalling? I'm hoping that one day he, too, can slow down and enjoy the ride.

Life really is a journey, not a destination!

Parents Aren't Perfect

● ●

Like most of us, I grew up putting my parents on the proverbial pedestal. But after almost four decades, I came to a shocking realization: My dad is not perfect. Brace yourself: Yours probably isn't, either. It's possible that fathers do not always know best. The horror!

You've probably sensed that I am a spirited, energetic and emotional person. Dad has told me that my "rampant enthusiasm," shall we say, sometimes works to my detriment. I can be overbearing. I am aware of this now and work on being calmer and more refined. My dad, on the other hand, is a reserved, pensive and wise man. Naturally, he wishes I possessed more of those qualities and dog-paddled quietly in his end of the gene pool. I feel bad that I cannot be as level-headed as he wants me to be, but it's just not natural to me. I like to backflip or belly-flop into the deep end and flail around. I'm very gung-ho and because dad isn't a fan of in-your-face intensity, I would often question myself.

Then my best friend, Dianne, who has that rare combination of wisdom and excitability, taught me one of my most valuable lessons.

We are teeing off on the second hole of the golf course when she says to me, "Hey, isn't that your mom and dad playing behind us?"

I look back and see my parents teeing up on the first hole with another couple. Dang. It had been so much fun up until now! Dianne and I have been talking and giggling freely. I whisper, "Oh man, I hope he didn't hear me laughing because I'll get in trouble for being too loud again."

Dianne is well aware of the situation. "Heather, why would you try and be like your dad?" She smiles and in a joking fashion adds, "If you were like him, I wouldn't hang out with you. It would be too boring!"

I can't help but laugh a bit, too. My never-ending quest to be the "He-Heather" that my dad wants me to be has been deemed unacceptable by my best friend. Could that mean that being "Me-Heather" would have been okay all along? The thought is foreign to me, almost sacrilegious.

"But I have always thought that my dad was right," I acknowledge, confused. "I am too boisterous."

"Heather," Dianne chuckles, "parents aren't perfect, you know. I learned that when I was twenty years old. It's about time you did, too!"

I realize in this life-changing moment that it's fine

to be "Me-Heather": a bubbly, outgoing thirty-seven-year old woman, not a wise, reserved seventy-year-old man. My friends are also vibrant people, which is why we gravitate to each other. So what is so wrong with just being "Me-Heather"? Nothing. Absolutely nothing.

Dianne and I continue playing as light-heartedly— and yes, probably as loudly—as we began. Her passing comment made it a game-changing game for me.

Criminal Behaviour

• •

I have a person I think of as a friend, who is a member at my golf club. We tee off together regularly, have a good rapport, kid around and share stories about our lives off the course. With all due modesty, and only because it's pertinent to the story, I am going to have to say here that I'm a better golfer than she is, so she often asks me for tips. I always spend whatever time it takes to coach her with her swing, read greens better, focus and so on. It can be a time-consuming process, and occasionally I even meet her for remedial help at the golf range. I am very proud of my patience in assisting her, even if it does sometimes detract from my own game. I like helping her.

So imagine my surprise when today, just as I'm due to tee off in a club tournament, she scampers over, asks me to explain something about her grip, and then basically flips out when I politely tell her I can't, I just don't have the time right this second. As she angrily strides away, she whips her head around (I think she could have managed the full Exorcist three hundred and sixty degrees!) and practically spits out, "Thanks for nothing."

I am so stunned that I have no idea what to do. I notice that the rest of my foursome and other nearby golfers are watching with disapproval as she stomps away. My jaw drops, my stomach sinks, and now I have to tee off in a tournament? Fanfreakintastic. I help this chick all of the time; how could she possibly be so disrespectful and rude at this moment, in front of our peers? How humiliating.

She ignores me the next two times I bump into her at the clubhouse. I do not go out of my way to speak to her.

I relay the story to Jennifer at our next appointment.

"So what do I do, Jennifer?"

"It's tough when relationships are off kilter. You were clearly shocked by her response and were hurt and felt underappreciated."

"I give a lot of my time to her. Now I feel like I am being taken advantage of! It's like one wrong move and she'll snap!"

"What feels like the correct way to handle this, Heather?"

"Set a more solid boundary with her."

"And what would that entail?"

"Well, she hasn't spoken to me since she was so rude to me, so I'm definitely not going to approach her first.

She has done this before and eventually always starts to ask for help again and we resume our friendship. This time, I have to put on the brakes because the way she treated me was totally unacceptable."

"If you know you're going to be friends again, you have to show her that she cannot treat you like a doormat. So yes, you do have to put a stronger boundary in place."

"And what would that entail?" I shoot back. I just love pulling a Jennifer on Jennifer!

She acknowledges my mimicry with a smile and proceeds to answer my question. "Often people appreciate knowing the amount of time that you have available to offer them. If you prepare them in advance, maybe let them know you have to leave for another appointment in fifteen minutes or whatever your constraint is, they won't feel surprised or upset when you have to head out or move onto something else without bringing total closure to whatever they're discussing or doing with you."

"Got it, but isn't that a bit rude? I'd feel like I was cutting them short."

"How so?"

"Well, first of all, as you know, I don't like to say no and go against the grain. Second, she is not used to this, and she very well might not like this change in my behaviour. Generally, I like being helpful, so it would feel awkward to me to tell her I only have ten minutes for her. It's contrary to my nature."

"Ahhh. Well said. It's a matter of finding the win-win situation here—the balance between being helpful versus being taken advantage of."

"I'll give it a shot. I don't want to be treated poorly by her again. It's simply not okay to act the way she did with me or with anyone. It's criminal!"

"Heather, setting boundaries and limits is an important life skill. It is not bad manners to speak the truth as long as you're articulating yourself in a kind and non-hurtful way."

Over time, I suppose I'll get used to setting boundaries. I'll just make sure I don't do it when my golfing buddy has a nine iron in her hand.

Gossip Girls

Ohhh, I love gossip. Good, juicy gossip. Nice, succulent tidbits. No wonder there are hit TV shows about it! We all love to gossip; we just don't want to be the subject of it. And since I have been the subject of it in the past (you're shocked, I'm sure), I swore that I would never again get involved in those delicious, subversive little chats about others. Unfortunately, I just had a mini-relapse after several months of biting my tongue raw.

After my golfing "frenemy" was rude with me, another golfer approached me on the links to complain about her. I felt validated. I wasn't the only one who had been treated unacceptably. Awesome. I have someone on my side. I listen for a while, nodding so enthusiastically I feel like a bobblehead, and then I leap right into the fray.

"And do you know what she said about you last week?" I ask, almost giddy with excitement.

"No, what?" My partner in crime's face perks up. Or I like to think it does. She might in fact look apprehensive. But I am unstoppable now; I have dirt and I am going to dish it. "Well, remember when you were giving her some tips on the tenth tee?"

"Yes…" My new supporter is totally engrossed in this slaughter now.

"Well, after the game she said that if you could drive a ball as well as you drive her crazy, you would be club champion." I gasp. "Isn't that awful?"

"What a she-devil!"

"I know," I reply, but my gossip high suddenly crashes. There's a sinking feeling in the pit of my stomach. I know very well that I should not have shared that information. Gossiping always gets me into trouble. I walk away consoling myself that maybe this time will be different; maybe she didn't even really hear exactly what I said. Maybe she will find it funny or just forget about it. Yes. It will blow over and never come up again. She knows I relayed it in the spirit of sharing and camaraderie. We have a bond in our disapproval of the other woman. It almost feels good.

Only twenty-four hours later, however, my new ally and I bump into our "frenemy" at the clubhouse. There is the usual exchange of pleasantries, and then she asks us if we'd like to join her for a drink on the patio. "Umm, sure," I say, tentatively.

"Not me," my gossip partner declines, staring at her

hard. "I'm pretty sure I would drive you crazy. I've been told I'm good at that."

Oh no, I'm in hot water. The look I get from both of them as they turn on their heels and clip away in their cleats tells me I won't be having a drink with either one anytime soon.

I share my mini-relapse with Jennifer at our next appointment.

"It sucks when you disappoint yourself, doesn't it, Heather?"

"Big time," I sigh.

"Let's focus on the positive. You've clearly learned a valuable lesson: Digressions are going to happen. They're bound to. That's okay. At this point, all you can do is learn from them, and it sounds like you already have."

"But what do I do next time someone starts up some gossip with me, especially about someone I've had problems with myself?"

"There are so many options. What do your instincts tell you?"

"It's a tough one for me," I confess, "because part of me wants to be part of the talk, but another part of me knows the drama gets worse. There's almost always a fallout."

"It's a question of how you feel knowing you have just gossiped about someone, even if you don't get caught."

"Well, more often than not, I feel really crappy," I admit.

"Okay, so we have an answer to your situation. Simply and politely tell a gossiper that you don't want to hear about it."

"Yeah, and then they'll go away and gossip about how rude I am," I remark with a roll of my eyes.

"Heather, when you are really upset and you are talking with a friend, what is it that makes you feel better?"

"When they listen to me. You know, just listen." A light dawns. "Damn, Jennifer, why didn't I think of that in the moment? Why didn't I just listen to her? Why did I have to jump in?" I jokingly smack myself on the forehead. "Okay, but since I did jump in, what could I have done to rectify the situation?"

"You could have caught yourself, and apologized immediately, perhaps saying something like, 'Ach, competitive golfers, you find them everywhere. Let's not dwell on this.' If you were nervous about it being repeated, you could admit your realization that you shouldn't have gossiped and kindly ask that the information not be shared."

"I actually did email her saying that I should not have gotten involved; that I thought it would be taken as a joke and that we were just kidding around."

"And how did she reply to that?"

"She emailed me back something like: 'No, I guess you shouldn't have gotten involved,' and uh, I think she deleted me as a friend on Facebook."

"Ah ha, I have an important reminder for you, Heather."

Brother, I'm messing up left, right and centre. "And what's that?"

"If someone's feelings have been hurt or something's really sensitive, stop yourself from emailing and talk in person, because you cannot read emotion or sincerity in an email."

How could I have forgotten that? "Oh, I've made such a big mess of this!" I can feel the nachos I had for lunch churning in my stomach.

"Well, let's keep perspective. This is all repairable. But how could you have avoided all of this damage control?"

This is the final question on the test and I definitely know the answer. "By simply stating politely in the first place that I don't want to hear any gossip."

"Precisely."

"Arm"ing Yourself
for Happiness

● ●

I'm chatting with my girlfriend about how lucky we are to have all of the things in our lives that we do. I say to her, "You have a gorgeous family, a nice home, great friends, a wonderful personality and you're beautiful; what more could you ask for?"

"I don't like my arms," she retorts disapprovingly.

Is she serious? Wow, she is so charming inside and out, how can she possibly be critical of her arms? I know she means it, though, so I carefully respond, "I think your perception of them is twisted. Your arms are just fine."

"I have always been unhappy with them," she replies sincerely.

I can see this is a problem for her and I know that she is not meant to feel this way. I'm not too sure what the solution is, but I make a suggestion. "How about whenever you think 'I don't like my arms,' you switch to 'I love my arms' instead?"

She laughs. "Well, I could do that but I don't think it will help."

I take the problem to Jennifer. There has to be a solution for this.

"Heather, it's great that you were able to see that her body image had nothing to do with reality, but you were off the mark when you told her to try to convince herself that she loves her arms."

"It's all that I could think of, Jennifer. I didn't know what else to say. I guess I had a 'Doctor Phil' moment."

Jennifer smiles, "Where does true happiness come from, Heather?"

"Well, I know it doesn't come from being rake thin, that's for sure."

"True happiness comes from within. Now I might sound like a pop psychologist, but it's true."

"Oh dear; so what I said to her was illogical? How can someone feel true happiness through such a meaningless thing as telling themselves that they love their arms?"

"Exactly! Now let me show you this." Jennifer gets out a piece of paper and draws two circles, one inside the other. "Heather, genuine happiness comes from what you are inside, like your personality, your moral standards, what you believe in and perhaps your intellect." She writes these words in the inside circle.

"External things, like your body, how much money you make or what kind of car you drive will never give you authentic happiness." She writes these words on the outside circle.

"So it doesn't matter that she doesn't like her arms? Because I have to tell you, she really, really hates her arms. You should see the way she glares at them!"

"Instead of thinking 'I love my arms,' she needs to think 'I am much more than my body,' and focus on her internal qualities. If she continues to do that, eventually she will love herself as a whole, arms included."

"I'll let her know. I think she'll be able to do that." I can already envision my friend confidently wearing a sleeveless top, something she hasn't done for years. This will make a huge difference to her, with global warming and all!

"Heather, what are you thinking about right now?" Jennifer asks.

This has to be a trick question, but I will play along. "The conversation we're having."

"And what else?"

"I don't know. I'm just enjoying my time with you." I have no idea what she is getting at.

"And does anything that we are doing right now, or in any of our recent appointments, have to do with our weight or our arms or any part of our bodies that we are not satisfied with?"

"Nope."

"There you have it. We've transcended that. Maybe we can both help others do the same."

As always, Jennifer's point is clear and, as always, I leave with the solution.

Not Worth Crying Over

• •

I bound up the stairs after a great game of tennis only to find my friend Nichola, who is working at the front desk, shaking and in tears. I am truly concerned. "What's wrong, sweetie?"

"My life is terrible. Everything bad happens to me."

"What's the matter?" I ask, offering a tissue and expecting a life crisis.

"This lady just got furious with me because I couldn't remember if the squash court fees were $5.25 or $5.75. So she freaked and asked to speak to my manager."

I'm shocked; this cannot possibly be why she is crying. I look around for the straw that broke the camel's back. It's not on the floor. "Is there anything else?"

"Remember that guy I told you I have feelings for?"

"Yes."

"Well," she manages as she blows her nose, "he just totally cut me off and hasn't spoken to me in five days."

Phew; that's why she's upset. We can deal with this. I know all too well that even though this is no life crisis, it can feel like one. I've had the same heartbreak myself. I mean, I freak out if a guy doesn't get back to me on a BlackBerry in five minutes, let alone five days. I hope I can help her.

Nichola continues to tell me about the guy (or "rat bastard," as I think she called him) who has hurt her and I listen with genuine interest. Once she has wound down, I ask her, "What would you like to get from dating this guy?"

She thinks for a bit. "A relationship where we have a connection," she starts.

"Companionship and to be accepted and loved by someone..." I suggest.

"Just saying that I have a boyfriend!" she interrupts. "I mean, that really matters at my age!"

Oh my gosh, she sounds exactly like me. I've been there, done that, got the tear-stained tee-shirt. I want to help her.

"Well, remember you told me that sometimes he doesn't treat you very well," I remind her.

"Yeah, that really upsets me. He kind of takes me for granted. He assumes I'll be there if there's nothing better going on."

"So clearly, you being upset like this is not really about this particular guy because you even said yourself that he doesn't provide you with what you need."

"No, he doesn't. Or didn't," she remembers, tearing up again.

"There have got to be other places where you can get these needs met." Oh dear, I'm starting to sound like Jennifer! "Where can you get companionship?"

"From my friends."

"And where can you get acceptance, no matter what?"

"From my family."

"And a connection? Where can you get that?"

"From both of the above," she says after only a few seconds. I think a see a light bulb going on.

"And why do you think you 'need' to have a boyfriend, even a bad one?"

Now, the room has dimmed again. Nichola frowns at me. "It gives me confidence."

"You can't find confidence in someone else. No one else can give you that."

"Then where do I get it?"

"From yourself. That's the kicker: It's right inside you, and only you." Little does she know how vital this lesson is. She looks at me like I've just stepped off a ship. A spaceship.

"But how?" she demands.

"This is so weird, because you sound exactly like I used to."

"Really? Because you always seem so happy and confident."

Did she just say that? I know I feel the change inside

me but I guess it's showing on the outside now, too. Neat!

"One thing I've found is that if I consciously act with integrity and confidence, even if I don't really feel the confidence inside, it eventually wears off on me and I end up feeling really good about myself. You are how you act. You become how you act. You fake it until you make it, so to speak."

That's the truth and it's a pretty quick process. "And if you act like you don't need a boyfriend to feel confident, you eventually will be confident without one," I summarize.

"And if I am confident, or seem to be, I'm more likely to attract a boyfriend who will value me," she says with a smile. "Or I'll be happy without one, so it's a win-win. Thanks, Heather. I feel a million times better now."

Nice. Now if she could only figure out how much the squash-court fees are...

The Art of Flirting

• •

"I'm golfing with this guy on Friday and I'm so excited, Jennifer! I know he's interested in me, but how do I get him even more interested?"

She laughs, "You need to play a bit of a game of cat and mouse while you play that game of golf."

"Cat and mouse?"

"Yes, Heather, and you are not the cat!"

I am not the cat? But I so like to pounce! "Oh man, this is going to be hard," I mutter.

"Well, you don't want to seem desperate, so you need to lay low."

"What do you mean exactly?" I need every mouse tip that I can possibly get.

"Take this example. If one night your friends are going out and you know that, but they haven't invited you yet, what would you do?"

"I'd ask one of them if I could come," I say in a heart-beat.

"Oh, Heather, that is a classic example of being the cat. You don't want to do that. What if you waited until they asked you to come, instead of you asking them? How would that feel?"

"Oh dear, much better than inviting myself! Then I would be sure that they wanted me there."

"Exactly. So let's assume that this date goes well. Instead of you asking when you're going to see him again or play again, wouldn't you feel better waiting and having him ask you out for a second time?"

I agree that I would.

"Now on the date," she continues, "you're going to remember to ask him about himself, instead of talking all about yourself. A lesson you remember well," she grins.

"And sometimes, you don't even need to use words," she adds. "You can have good chemistry non-verbally with a gentle touch to his arm or a hand lightly on his back. You can also connect with him simply by the way you look at him."

I'm unconvinced. I'm more of a straight shooter than a flirter. "I hope I can do this," I sigh.

"It's one hundred and fifty percent in you."

Comments like this, from Jennifer, help me believe in myself because I know her belief in me is sincere. She never lies to me and she knows me inside and out. What other tips does she have for a neophyte mouse?

"Five minutes before you meet up with him, take a

deep breath, ground yourself and assure yourself that you are worthy of anyone," she advises. "Remember: Be a class act."

A class act is still exactly what I am striving for, so this makes sense to me. I will "fake it till I make it," a lesson from long ago that continues to serve me well. Concepts that initially seemed "weird" or "airy-fairy" to me are now accessible and intertwine. I "get" them and I use them.

Needless to say, the date went well. And he never did figure out why, on our next one, I laughed when he ordered a cheese appetizer.

Text, Text, Tsk, Tsk

I once heard that a lesson will keep repeating itself until it is learned. Well, I guess I have not learned this texting lesson yet because it keeps coming back to haunt me. I remain convinced that the BlackBerry is addictive. I get physical shakes and break out into a sweat if mine is not immediately at hand. There must be a twelve-step program or support group out there somewhere. Maybe it's called CA, for CrackBerrys Anonymous. Hey, wait a minute: I am a CA, as in Chartered Accountant! This addiction must have been my destiny.

I get into a conversation with an old boyfriend—on my BlackBerry, of course. We are trying to figure out why it could or couldn't work out between us, with me texting him on his cell phone. Anyway, you can see where this is going. You know that I know it is lethal to text about emotions. But I think to myself, this time it will be different because I'm talking to Adam, who never argues. He talks things through with me and would never do any harm. So I convince myself that this is a conversation we—and we alone—are able to have by text messaging.

I still have feelings for him and luckily we have stayed friends. I text him: "Are you available tonight? Would it be possible to meet up?"

No reply. Two minutes later, still no reply. Seven minutes later, nope, no reply. Seven hours later, nothing. Nada. Zip. Zilch. I spend the night a slave to my BlackBerry waiting for Adam to text me back. He doesn't. I'm hurt. I can't sleep.

The next morning, I tell my girlfriend the story and she says, "Hey, maybe he isn't such a class act after all."

"I guess not," I have to agree.

I grow increasingly frustrated as a few more minutes or nano-seconds drag on. It's time for one of my infamous knee-jerk reactions. I fire off a text: "Don't you think that was a little rude not replying last night? What kind of friend does that?"

He responds: "My phone went dead so by the time I got your message it was 11:30 p.m. and I didn't want to wake you. And I am just finishing up a breakfast meeting. That kind of friend."

Nailed again. Man, I feel dreadful now. I spent the evening worrying that I was being ignored and now I've alienated a person who was actually being sensitive to my needs.

I am now writing on an adhesive label that I will attach to the face of my BlackBerry: Don't make assumptions.

Just Stay Out of It

. . . .

"Jennifer, I'm caught in a situation and I don't know what to do."

"Tell me about it."

"Well, I have these two great friends that I really like and I thought they would be a good couple. I set them up on a blind date."

Jennifer shakes her head, smiling in a knowing manner. "Matchmaking. Oh, boy. I can predict where this is going!"

"Well, they did spend some time together, but it turns out that she likes him more than he likes her. I know because they've both told me how they feel. Now, I don't know what to do. I feel bad for my girlfriend, Moira, because I know my guy friend, Jeff, is just stringing her along. To make things worse, he asked me to keep his feelings in confidence."

"What have you done so far?"

"I've just listened to them both. I know it's best to stay out of it."

"Perfect!" Jennifer looks relieved. "Can you talk to Jeff and suggest he talk directly to Moira?"

"I suppose so, but what if he doesn't want to?" And he won't.

"Well, Heather, direct communication is always best. As it stands, if you get involved it will become a triangle between the three of you and no one will know the truth. It's up to them to communicate with each other, not you. If you do get involved, someone is bound to get hurt."

"Probably me," I mutter. "Okay, I agree. I won't take on their problems."

I get home and see that my voice mail is flashing. Uh-oh. Am I too late? I press the sound button. "Heather, this is Moira. Can you call me please," she requests icily. "As soon as you get this." Click. Yep. She's angry.

I pick up the phone with apprehension. "Hi, Moira," I say as cheerily as I can when she answers. "Gee, how the heck are you?"

I'm not a happy camper. Jeff has told her that he's not interested in her, but he has also told her that I have known that for a few days. What a chump!

"Heather, why didn't you tell me?" she demands.

"Moira, you are not going to believe this, but I just spent my entire therapy session talking about this situation. The whole sixty minutes. I really didn't know what to do. What I learned is that I needed to stay out of it and I was right to stay out of it. I'm really sorry. But on the up side," I conclude, attempting some humour, "I'm not going to bill you for my session."

That elicits a small snort of laughter. "Well, thanks for that. I guess I'm a bit flattered that you talked about me with your therapist. I completely thought you were being mean, but yeah, okay, I agree it's generally best not to involve yourself in other people's relationships."

"No kidding!" My days of playing Cupid are over.

Being "Normal"

•••••••••••••••••••••••••••••••••

I'm disoriented as I wake up this morning. Am I still in a hospital? I look around my bedroom groggily. Phew; no, that nightmare was over years ago. I'm so thankful to be home in my own cozy room and my own cozy bed.

I say to myself, "Today I'm going to have the best day of my life."

My friend Evelyn tells me that she has been watching me "wake up" throughout my recovery. She says I have been like Rip Van Winkle, wanting to grab hold of life and make up for my many missed years and experiences.

As I'm brushing my teeth, I play my usual game. I'm going to name five things that I am grateful for. What will they be today? I am blessed to have such an abundance to choose from.

I pull up my jeans. The zipper resists. I breathe in, suck in, and voila. That's a new one! At least I didn't have to lie down on the bed to wrangle with them! Still, they are definitely tighter today than they were last time.

Hmm…wait: My period should be coming in a few days. I chalk it up to that. I know this is normal. I don't need to hit a panic button. This is yet another thing to be thankful for. I am accepting that my body changes as the days of the month pass, and sometimes even from morning to night, especially after some of my mom's apple pie.

At work I enjoy my file, and my boss and I have agreed on a reasonable timeline for me to do a quality job. I feel confident and self-assured. Now that is cool! My co-workers tell me that the changes in me are astonishing. I am more engaged, more refined and clearly experiencing the joy of life.

I get home from work and stop dead in my tracks. I forgot my BlackBerry at the office! To my delight, I feel relieved. A BlackBerry-free evening! Bliss! To think that once upon a time (okay, not all that long ago), I would have turned around and raced back to retrieve it—like its slave. I might even have driven through a few red lights and yes, parked in a spot for the handicapped on a frantic retrieval mission. Tsk, tsk… Bad, Heather, bad!

Dinner is at my mom's tonight, and woo-hoo, it is indeed apple pie for dessert again. Mmm… Thank you so much, Mom. I savour it and as usual she sends me home with a care package. I take it home and put it in the fridge. I go to bed feeling satisfied and thankful for such a lovely day. I enjoy my second piece of pie the next night. How simple and nice to experience that taste again and to think warm thoughts about my wonderful mom. She's the best. Even if she buys the pie, I say good for her for simplifying! All day every day now, I feel connected to people. I'm committed to a better way of living, with integrity and a truly positive outlook.

I finally "get it." There is no textbook, no formula, no magic for recovery. I only recovered when I stopped black-and-white thinking and discovered the colour grey—or, as Jennifer might say, the colour pink! I got to know myself and to understand my limits. I love that I now give myself approval to be the best "imperfect" me that I can be.

A very caring person once told me that, "Perfection is in the full acceptance of imperfection." Thank you, Jennifer. The fact that you believed in me was all that I needed to start believing in myself. And believing in myself—imperfections and all—turned out to be the only thing I needed all along.

What a great day. Thanks, Jennifer, for reminding me that extracting the positive is the best way to acquire a happy life. Now, I look back on my illness and realize that I would not be the person I am today had I not experienced the difficulties that I have. Now, I can fully appreciate (though maybe not fully understand) other people's struggles (we all have them) and I can empathize. I have taken the good out of my illness and every day I look forward to more Life 101 lessons. Keep 'em coming, world, because I'm always up for learning!

I will swing at the curve balls life inevitably throws us. But I'm determined to throw fewer and fewer at myself.

Reflections

● ●

"Heather, I can't believe our sessions are over. This has been a true ride."

"Has it ever. I've had some painful discoveries about myself, but they've been balanced with your great insights and even our laughs together."

"We have had some laughs." Jennifer smiles warmly. "I think you really solidified your life learning by writing your book. What do you think?"

"Without a doubt, Jennifer, but really, the book is as much about you as it is about me. I will never, ever be able to thank you enough for all you've done for me, for all you've shown me."

"It has been a true pleasure to see how much you have grown, Heather. I feel so lucky to have worked with you from the day you started treatment. Seeing your progress makes the work I do feel so worthwhile. You have turned your whole life around!"

"You're going to make me cry."

"You should. Tears of joy!"

I'm holding myself back. But then Jennifer looks at me with such kindness that my eyes do well up and the tears begin to fall. I realize that she has tears in her eyes as well. I've always known that she has believed in me. I've always known that she genuinely cares. But right now I also know her care for me is not because I was her client; it is because she respects me as a whole, as the perfect imperfect me.

"Heather, I can see you are thinking there. Do you want to share your thoughts?"

"Yes," I manage to utter as I pull out some tissue and blow my nose with a Canada Goose honk. "Oh, how unlady like!" I exclaim and we laugh together. "I guess the best way to sum up my feelings right now is that I'm overwhelmed with happiness and appreciation for having you in my life."

"When we met, Heather, did you envision yourself here today?"

"I was hoping when we starting working together in your practice that my future was going to be bright and that I would regain my health, but I certainly never envisioned writing about it."

"I'm not sure you will remember this, but the first day I met you, you told me about your tennis career. You filled me in on how you became a national champion. Do you remember?"

"I don't, actually. How insecure that I needed to share

that on our first meeting!"

"Okay, okay, I'll sum up." Jennifer is chuckling. "I asked you a simple question. I asked if you could redirect the energy that you put into your tennis and compel it toward a happy and healthy life."

"Oh, I do remember that! I know I said yes, with some reservations!"

"That's right! But you opened yourself to the possibility that things could be different. You put your focus and intentions on living a fulfilling life. You walked your extra long, extra shaky suspension bridge to solid ground."

"And on the other side, I have found closeness with my family that fills me up. I've learned to have great fun with my dad and not take him too seriously and to trust my own judgement. Gosh, I've learned so many things: to slow down and truly take in life, to stand up for myself and set healthy boundaries, to listen to what others want, to not be so persistent..." I'm running out of the fingers I'm counting on, but I have more to go. "I've polished my communication skills, rounded out my professionalism, learned to love completely and with genuine empathy..." My voice trails off.

Wow. I really have turned my life around. Or we have, she and I.

Jennifer concludes with the statement that will forever be my favourite: "I knew you could do it!"

Afterword

● ●

A long-time friend approaches me and says she has a "huge favour" to ask. "What's that?" I inquire.

"My colleague's daughter has been suffering from anorexia and bulimia for over a year now and she refuses to get help. She says she's fine but her family and friends can see her withering away right in front of their eyes. Her mother is worried sick and doesn't know what to do."

I am reminded of the pain I put my own family through and feel a pang in my heart.

"How old is the girl?" I ask.

"Eighteen and I think you can help her because you've been there yourself and recovered so well. You are the only person I know who understands the struggle and how to beat it. The problem is, she refuses to talk to anyone."

"Tell her I completely understand and if she would like, I can meet her for coffee. Maybe it will help convince her if you tell her that I've been exactly where she is now."

"I was hoping you'd say I could share that. Thanks, Heather. I'll give it a try."

Two weeks later, I am standing in front of a beautiful brunette. She looks scared and tentative, a look I find all too familiar.

"Hi," I give her a warm smile as I sit down and join her. "My name is Heather." She doesn't reply. "I just want to make you feel comfortable," I say after a couple of minutes of silence. "There's no need for you to say anything if you don't want to. I can simply tell you my story."

"Thanks, because I don't really want to talk," she declares bluntly.

"I completely understand," I reassure her. And I do.

After about forty-five minutes of what I hope has been an engaging monologue, she starts to share. Phew; I've made her comfortable. I listen carefully and we discuss how we can both relate to similar destructive behaviours and thoughts.

She then asks reluctantly, "Heather, can I tell you something that I haven't told anyone?"

"Of course, and whatever it is, I'm sure I've heard worse," I encourage her. "As you know, there's no judgement here."

"I've thrown up my dinner every day for the past year."

"And nobody has noticed?" I inquire casually.

"No. I'm really secretive about it."

"Okay." I mull this over. "Is it only once a day you do this?"

"Well, sometimes now it's twice. Like the other day, when I was out for lunch with some friends, they were bugging me that I don't eat. They ordered a pizza and so finally I had a piece just to get them off my back. I felt so awful after I ate it, I threw it up. And I couldn't keep anything down for the rest of the day."

"That one piece of pizza totally threw you off, didn't it?"

"You have no idea." Tears spring to her eyes.

"Oh, yes I do. And I know what to do about it."

"You do?" She seems surprised.

"Yep. Would you like to know?"

"Yes."

"First of all, it only gets worse once you start. Just like losing a few pounds becomes losing a few more pounds until it gets out of your control, throwing up occasionally becomes once a day, then twice a day; you can see where I'm going with this."

"Yes, that is what's happening to me." She looks miserable.

"Let's make a plan for now to keep you safe so that today, just today, you don't throw up."

She looks at me skeptically.

We spend thirty minutes making up an eating plan for the day that won't push her over the edge. All we want to do is break the cycle, just for one day: today.

Twenty-four hours of safety. Baby steps.

She likes the plan and she really likes it when I say, "I know you can do it."

She smiles broadly. "I think I can, too."

The next morning she texts me: "Heather, I did it!!! Yesterday, for the first time in a year, I didn't throw up. I'm so glad and I couldn't have done it without your help."

My heart swells and my eyes well up with tears.

I know you can do it! Sometimes those wonderful words of encouragement, first shared with me by Jennifer, are the first step on the path from hopeless and helpless to happy and healthy.

Acknowledgments

• •

There are so many people to thank for saving my life, and I mean literally *saving my life*. Dr. Staab, your willingness to work with me, your careful attention to my medical care and your patience have been outstanding. Thank you to Sonja and Jannine, my sisters, for too many things to even try to mention. To my friends, Eveline Gaede, Dianne Fisher, Jean Farhood, Sarah Lawless and my tennis coach Ed Andrulis, who stood by me during my most difficult times: Your genuine care, positivity and realism have kept me grounded. Mom and Dad, thank you for your endless support. Without you, I would not be here today. (And I do not simply mean because you gave birth to me!) I thank you for everything you have taught me throughout my life; I am so happy to have and enjoy you as my friends during my adulthood. Finally, I thank Jennifer Brighton, who is my true guardian angel. When I count by blessings, Jennifer, I count you twice.

This book is intended with the understanding that the author is not rendering psychological, medical or professional services. The information in this book is the author's own autobiography and is intended to provide helpful, hopeful and informative material on overcoming eating disorders and gaining self-esteem. It is not a replacement for professional medical or psychological advice. The names of people in this book have either been changed or are real with the individual's prior approval to be a part of this book. Some of the content is a combination of various individual events or persons.